"No matter what challenges you previously faced, this resource can help you reinvent your marriage and renew your love for each other. Great for all who want to make the rest of their marriage the best!"

Timothy Clinton, Ph.D.,
president, American Association of Christian Counselors

The Second Half of Marriage *is full of rich insights into marriage in later life and the many challenges and hopes it offers. There is great wisdom in this volume in a vital area of life that is too often ignored. It is a must read."*

John Gottman, Ph.D.,
marital researcher and author of
Why Marriages Succeed or Fail

"This should be required reading for every couple in the 'second half.' We highly recommend this resource in our mentoring program."

Drs. Les & Leslie Parrott,
co-directors of the Center for
Relationship Development, Seattle Pacific University
and authors of *Saving Your Marriage Before It Starts*

"We people of our proud, youth-oriented America tend to arrive at the maturing years of marriage with rusty relationships. The Arps' stiff scouring brush is a powerful anti-corrosive for 'Help, we're hitting bottom!' mid-lifers."

Howard and Jeanne Hendricks,
Distinguished Professor and Chairman
of the Center for Christian Leadership
Dallas Theological Seminary

RESOURCES BY DAVID AND CLAUDIA ARP

Books

10 Great Dates
Love Life for Parents
Suddenly They're 13!
Quiet Whispers from God's Heart for Couples
Marriage Moments
Family Moments

Video Curriculum

10 Great Dates
The Second Half of Marriage
PEP (Parents Encouraging Parents) Groups for Moms
PEP Groups for Parents of Teens

**For more information about Marriage Alive resources
or to schedule the Arps for a Marriage Alive Seminar
or other speaking engagements contact:**

Marriage Alive International
51 West Ranch Trail
Morrison, CO 80465
Phone: (888) 690-6667
Email: mace@marriagealive.org
Website: www.marriagealive.com

The Second Half of Marriage

of Marriage

*Facing the Eight Challenges
of the Empty-Nest Years*

DAVID AND CLAUDIA ARP

ZONDERVAN™

GRAND RAPIDS, MICHIGAN 49530

ZONDERVAN™

The Second Half of Marriage
Copyright © 1996 by David and Claudia Arp

Discussion guide © 1998 by David and Claudia Arp

Requests for information should be addressed to:

Zondervan, *Grand Rapids, Michigan 49530*

Library of Congress Cataloging-in-Publication Data

Dave, Arp.
    The second half of marriage : facing the eight challenges of the empty-nest years
  / David and Claudia Arp.
      p.   cm.
    Includes bibliographical references (p.   ).
    ISBN: 0-310-21935-3 (softcover)
    1. Marriage.   2. Empty nesters.   3. Married people.   4. Marriage—Religious
aspects—Christianity.   I. Arp, Claudia.   II. Title.
HQ734.A6895   1996
646.7'8—dc20   96-18553
                                                  CIP

Published in association with the literary agency of Alive Communications, Inc., 7680 Goddard Street, Suite 200, Colorado Springs, CO 80920

This book is a resource for marriage enrichment, not a substitute for needed professional counseling. If some of the exercises contained in this book raise issues for you or your spouse that cannot be easily resolved, we urge you to seek professional help.

The names and identifying details of the individuals in the stories within have been changed to protect their privacy.

Interior design by Sherri L. Hoffman

Printed in the United States of America

---

02 03 04 05 /❖ DC/ 12 11 10 9 8 7 6

To our loved sons and daughters-in-law,
Jarrett and Laurie, Joel and Jeanne, and Jonathan and Autumn,
who enrich the second half of our marriage,
may you face the challenge of marriage with courage, faith,
and anticipation that the best is yet to be.

Contents

Part Four: The Marriage Challenge

From Dr. Vera Mace: A Message to a Couple of Book Browsers Who Are Wondering, *Shall We Read It?*

Y̲ou are going on a journey—a journey governed by the inscrutable passage of time, a journey into that part of life known as the second half. You may try to soften its implications and demands by pretending that you are not really there yet, but as the years pass, "yet" will be wiped out and your journey will lead you to your goal in the second half of marriage.

Here is a book from many fellow travelers, led by Dave and Claudia Arp. They hold out their hands to you and say, "We are going the same way. Come travel with us." I would urge you to accept their invitation. Perhaps you think you are not *prepared* to journey with them. In this case, preparation doesn't matter one whit. With their hands outstretched, they want to share with you how to prepare for and make the most of your journey. Perhaps for some, your marriages are shadowed by past inadequacies or failure. Here in this book you can learn to understand and accept these past experiences and use them to make your journey into the second half of marriage richer in relationships and fuller and happier in every way.

As I reflect on my journey through the second half of marriage, I realize that whereas the living of the first half was so much a response to circumstances, children, jobs, homes, what country we should live in, families, wartime conditions, and the like, the second half offered a new *freedom to choose, to change, to seek fulfillment* for our hopes and dreams. (How I identify with the McCrackens' story!) Now in my nineties and widowed after fifty-seven years of a wonderful marriage, I know beyond a shadow of a doubt that the second half of marriage can be a very privileged time when

> All we have willed or hoped or dreamed of good shall exist;
> Not its semblance, but itself.
>
> —Robert Browning

Why not choose to join the traveler couples in this book?

—Vera Mace

A Personal Note from Claudia and Dave

Parenting three energetic and impish sons wasn't always a breeze—it was more of a tornado. But with a few good parenting principles, lots of laughter, God's grace, and over twenty years of forced labor, we survived. It was only after our last son left for college that the reality of our new situation hit us. We were now in the empty nest. No more late nights waiting for the last child to climb in through his bedroom window. No need to wonder who is coming home for dinner (and if fifteen pizzas will be enough). We were once again in control of our home, our schedules, and ourselves—so we thought!

It didn't take long to realize we had some work to do on our marriage. Our roles and responsibilities were turned upside down. Claudia didn't have to coordinate Jonathan's tennis tournaments, and there were no mandatory soccer games or impromptu teenage parties at the Arps'. Our family's typical hectic and crisis-filled rhythm was disrupted. With no children at home, our schedules filled up with writing projects, speaking engagements, and long-overdue home improvements. (It was time to fix that shower leak!) We went from a child-centered marriage to an activity-centered one, still with little time and energy for each other. We knew we needed help, so we began to look for some expert advice.

While scouring libraries, bookstores, and our personal collection of marriage enrichment resources, we discovered that there was very little practical material specifically addressing the second half of marriage. We were incredulous. With the recent emphasis on maintaining a healthy, fulfilling, and productive second half of life, we thought there must be scads of advice on sustaining and improving the second half of marriage. There isn't.

Now, we have never been a couple to back down from a challenge. And for two writers with no children in the house, this was the perfect challenge for us. We decided to research second-half marriages and develop a successful strategy for improving our own relationship. We had seen couples whose marriages blossomed in the second half. And sadly, we had witnessed far too many marriages fail in the second half. We wanted to know what the essential ingredients to a lifelong, happy, and loving relationship were and how to avoid becoming an unfortunate statistic.

Conventional wisdom indicated that many couples stayed together while children were the focus of the relationship; when the children left home, so did the reason for staying in the relationship. Our own personal experience gave support to the theory that marital satisfaction is at its lowest during the teen years. We always loved each other and did our best to support one another, but we were often overwhelmed by the demands of our three adolescent sons. There was little energy left to devote to our friendship, let alone intimacy. But we also knew that one day our children would be gone. We would have to redefine our relationship, renew the love, and reconnect a close companionship that had characterized the beginning of our marriage more than twenty-five years before.

Since we have worked in the family-life education field for more than twenty years, we were quite comfortable interviewing couples to discover the common areas of concern and common traits of success. So we began our search for information among our friends, our associates, and the participants in our Marriage Alive seminars. We developed a survey designed to determine the keys to a successful second-half marriage.

Our research revealed eight themes within a second-half marriage. One is the need to transition from a child-focused marriage to a more partner-focused marriage. Without the children as buffers, couples face the challenge of redefining their marriage. Either it becomes more intimate or it slowly disintegrates. Another is the task of relearning how to communicate and effectively deal with conflict and anger. A third is the challenge of adjusting to changing roles with aging parents and adult children. All eight are discussed in part 2.

We were encouraged to observe that those couples who successfully made it through the empty nest passage achieved a higher level of marital satisfaction. We developed eight marital challenges for creating and maintaining a successful second-half marriage. These challenges form the framework for this book. We are convinced that if you surmount these challenges, your marriage will be successful. To provide practical help, we have included Marriage Builder exercises to help you identify your own marital challenges and potential strategies for success.

Since nothing is quite as helpful as real-life experience, we've liberally sprinkled our own marital struggles—as well as helpful tips from some of our survey participants—throughout the book. Finally, we've included the remarkable story of our friends John and Sarah McCracken. While discussing this project with them, we discovered that their marriage had hit a brick wall when their children left home. And in their pursuit of a better second-half marriage, they had overcome each of these challenges and had transformed their relationship into a more personal and fulfilling one.

In part 3 you will get to know John and Sarah McCracken, who have lived through this process and met the challenges remarkably well. You'll see the inner workings of their marriage as they transitioned from raising three children to facing the empty nest and on to enjoying retirement. You will observe how they developed "we-ness" in their relationship as they moved from a traditional marriage to a companionship marriage. Their names and a few details have been altered, but their story is true and can be an encouragement to all of us.

We have crafted part 4 to be your own personal marriage challenge. Over the years of our marriage, we have confirmed that real growth involves more than knowledge. You must translate that knowledge into experience.

As you go through *The Second Half of Marriage*, you will have the opportunity to transform your own marriage, to make midcourse adjustments, and to reconnect with one another in a more personal way. Of course, we realize that at this stage of life, many couples are in their second marriages. The encouraging news is that whether it's literally your second marriage or it's the second half of your first marriage, your marriage can be improved. Even if your relationship is distant, you can choose to move closer and your love can mature. You can make the rest the best!

PART ONE

Getting Ready for the Second Half

Grow old along with me. The best is yet to be;
The last of life, for which the first was made.
Our times are in His hand who saith, "A whole
   I planned,
Youth shows but half; Trust God: See all, nor
   be afraid!"

—Robert Browning

"Help! I'm Having a Midlife Marriage"

The hard part is staying in love—that is, keeping intimacy alive, even growing closer—through the years.

—Dr. Georgia Witkin[1]

W e'll never forget the day we dropped our youngest son, Jonathan, off at college. It was a beautiful, crisp day in Wheaton, Illinois. All of Jonathan's boxes and plastic garbage bags full of clothes, and most of his earthly possessions, were safely in his freshman dormitory room.

As we said our farewells, Jonathan looked so young and vulnerable, but we knew he was ready to face the academic and social challenges that college was sure to present. We weren't so sure about ourselves and the challenges waiting for us. Slowly we got into our car, backed out of the parking lot, and waved our last good-byes. As we turned out of the Wheaton College campus and began the ten-hour trip back to Knoxville, Tennessee, we knew we were entering uncharted waters.

Claudia, the navigator, asked, "Dave, do you want to go via Louisville, Kentucky, or Cincinnati, Ohio? It's quicker to go through Louisville, but there's not as much traffic the other way."

"Why rush home?" Dave answered. "There's no one there! We don't even have to make it home tonight!"

"You're right," Claudia said. "But it just feels so strange not to be needed at home. Maybe we should go directly home. I've been waiting years to go through our house with Lysol!"

"OK, if that's what you want to do, but from now on we don't have to rush. Personally, I can't wait to get home and get reacquainted with our empty house and my lovely wife," Dave responded with a gleam in his eyes.

At last we were entering the "empty nest" stage of family life. Jonathan's flight from the nest was preceded by those of his two older brothers, who were already married and on their own. Suddenly it was just the two of us.

As the miles clicked by, Claudia smiled and thought about how differently she and Dave were facing the empty nest. Dave, true to his laid-back temperament, breathed a sigh of relief that seemed to say, "We made it!" Claudia, the introspective one, wondered, *How does this affect our relationship?* and *What do we do now?* Both of us sensed that this was a transitional time in our lives. Our twenty-five-year-plus marriage was teetering on the brink of new challenges, obstacles, and opportunities for growth.

As we talked about our empty house, we realized how quickly the first half of our marriage (the parenting years) had gone by. From the baby- and toddler-years, with their endless miles of diapers, to wall-to-wall Legos and peanut-butter-covered doorknobs, to soccer leagues, skinned knees, and water balloon fights, to the exasperating adolescent years—our life had zipped by. Now, almost caught unawares, we faced a new era. No longer would life at the Arps' rotate around our three sons and our parenting responsibilities. As we sped toward our empty nest, we felt apprehensive.

BEGINNING THE SECOND HALF

In the coming weeks, the color of the leaves was not the only thing that was changing. Our familiar hectic family routine was suddenly replaced with new vistas and opportunities. We both jumped into fall activities with a can-do attitude that quickly took over our calendar and lives. Suddenly all the things we had delayed until the kids left home were now possibilities. In record time, we accepted too many conferences, writing projects, and speaking engagements. Claudia continued with her parenting programs across the country.

There was little time left over for us to deal with our marriage "back burner" agenda—those things that were important to our marriage, things we had ignored and had let accumulate over the years. Signs of aging were appearing. For instance, our backs told us that we were not bionic and that they needed more tender loving care. And our romantic candle was flickering uncomfortably near the end of the wick. The lack of privacy, the exhaustion, and the emotional drain of teenagers in our home had taken a toll on our love life. Our own social life was practically nonexistent. We had lost touch with our friends, who were overwhelmed with their own teenagers, careers, and fast-paced lives. And now we were taking our hours and days, which had previously been occupied with parenting responsibilities, and packing them with other activities and challenges. Rather than moving from a child-focused to a partner-focused marriage, we were quickly moving to an activity-focused relationship.

Here we were, new inductees into the empty nest and just as tired and overcommitted as ever. One morning we were both totally exhausted. As we sat at our breakfast table, staring at each other over two cups of coffee, we agreed that something had to give—and we didn't want it to be our marriage. We knew we needed some time away to sort things out.

A SENTIMENTAL JOURNEY

For years, we had looked forward to the second half of marriage and often talked about taking an empty-nest trip—a trip during which we could regroup and initiate the second half of our marriage. We had always wanted to visit New England, so as we had dreamed about our empty nest, we had dreamed of seeing the fall foliage in Vermont, Maine, and New Hampshire. That morning, we discussed our dream and decided to turn it into reality. In a few weeks we were to lead our Marriage Alive seminar for a church in the Washington, DC, area. So we resolved that after our seminar was over, we would head north.

At last we were in the car, driving toward Camden, Maine! Getting away as a couple was not a new experience for us. Over the years, we had taken little getaways, telling our sons it was for their own good. After all, we were so much nicer when we returned. But this was different. We didn't have to worry about things at home. We were free to concentrate on us, and it felt very good.

The first couple of days, we had no agenda except to relax and enjoy being together. We knew from past experience that right after leading our Marriage Alive seminars was usually a time of vulnerability for us. We use so much emotional energy helping other couples that we need some time to get restored ourselves. So we slept late each morning and enjoyed a delicious breakfast at the quaint bed-and-breakfast where we were staying. One morning the owners even sang for us!

Being in a more relaxed setting was a catalyst for romance. We were definitely unwinding until Claudia said, "Dave, this is great fun, but it's time we take a closer look at our marriage. Let's spend today taking stock of our marriage."

Dave, knowing Claudia quite well, said, "That means you want to take a long walk." Her big smile let him know he was on the right track.

We don't know what it is about walking, but that's when we communicate best, so we took a hike on the coast of Maine. The cool, brisk wind and misty spray from the waves energized us as we surveyed the state of our marriage.

A MARRIAGE CHECKUP

Away from all our responsibilities and with no one else around, we were free to talk about our marriage and where we wanted it to go in the future. As we ushered in the second half of our marriage, we defined our goals. First we needed to reconnect as a couple, redefine our relationship, and let go of some of our unrealistic dreams. We simply couldn't do all the things we had planned to do when the children grew up—plus, to be honest, we didn't have the energy.

Marriage Assets

As we began the process of evaluating our relationship, we took a hard look at our marriage. "What are the best aspects of our marriage?" Claudia asked.

"Well," said Dave, "first, we survived parenting three boys! That should count for something! We laugh together, we really like each other, and we enjoy being together."

"We're best friends, and both of us are committed to our marriage," Claudia added.

Other things we listed were our pioneering spirit, our common values and interests, and a communication system that works (most of the time!). Since we work as family-life educators, we spend an unusually large amount of time together. Even though the lines between professional and personal can be blurry, our working together has been more of an asset than a liability. We care about marriages in general and about our marriage specifically. We agreed that our most important assets were our commitment to God and to each other, our commitment to growth, and our bullheaded determination to make our marriage work even when we experience conflict.

Our faith in God is the foundation for our marriage. We define our marriage as a partnership with each other and with God. Years ago we chose Ecclesiastes 4:9–12 as a theme for our marriage. It describes what we want our marriage relationship to look like:

> Two are better than one, because they have a good return for their work: If one falls down, his friend can help him up. But pity the man who falls and has no one to help him up! Also, if two lie down together, they will keep warm. But how can one keep warm alone? Though one may be overpowered, two can defend themselves. A cord of three strands is not quickly broken.

Our vow, made many years ago, to stay together "till death do us part" was a solemn vow. For us, divorce has never been an option. But there are many times we let each other down—like when Dave doesn't keep up with the time and is late again or when Claudia falls asleep when Dave has planned a romantic evening for us. It's times like these when we look to our faith in God to keep our cord strong. In our marriage, we like to think about Dave being one strand, Claudia being one strand, and God's Holy Spirit being the third strand that holds it all together when our individual strands are frayed.

Our relationship with God empowers us to forgive each other and to be willing to say, "I'm sorry. Will you please forgive me?" No human relationship offers the closeness and intimacy of the marriage relationship, but with it also comes the greatest opportunity for anger and conflict. So along with our faith in God comes our determination to learn how to cope with anger and make our marriage work.

Marriage Liabilities

Next on our agenda was looking at our marriage liabilities. As we faced our second half, what were our stumbling blocks? The first thing we thought of was time pressure. We simply didn't have enough hours in each day to do all the things we wanted to do. But then we realized that this was just a symptom. Our real liability was our tendency to overcommit ourselves, to procrastinate, and to say yes when we should say no.

Where was all that time we were supposed to have after the kids left home? Unfortunately, we had filled it up with more commitments and more deadlines. How could we control our tendency toward being workaholics? It was hard for us to find the boundary between work and home. We had already listed our work in marriage enrichment as a marriage asset, but we began to see that it could also be listed as a liability.

Our commitment to helping other couples' marriages and families sometimes infringes on the time we need just for us. For instance, when we wrote the book *52 Dates for You and Your Mate*, we wanted to help couples spend quality time together having fun and building relationships. As we were promoting the book, we spent one entire Valentine's Day doing media interviews! In the final interview of that long day, our friend Jim Warren, host of the national radio program *Prime Time America*, asked us, "Dave, Claudia, tell us about your last date."

We had to admit that we had been so busy encouraging other people to date their mates, we had let our own dating habit go by the wayside. For sure, it had been several months since we'd had a real date—and sadly, neither of us could remember when it was or what we did.

A second liability for us was the fact that parenting adolescents had drained us emotionally. We had worked hard at preparing our sons for adulthood, but now we needed to release them emotionally and invest some of that emotional energy back into our marriage.

We just didn't have the emotional reserve of days gone by, and it was easier for us to react to each other's little irritations. Like when one of us (and we won't say who) leaves clothes in the bathroom or leaves used Kleenex just lying around or forgets to turn the light off or the heat down.

Other liabilities were lack of planning, health issues (like our backs), unrealistic expectations, misplaced priorities, and lack of focus.

DREAM, DREAM, DREAM

That evening in Camden, Maine, we ate dinner in a little restaurant on the pier. The warmth of the fireplace took the chill off the room, and the candlelight put a glow on the whole conversation. We felt ten thousand miles away from Knoxville. Fully aproned and equipped with multiple napkins, we ate lobster and continued to talk about our marriage. How could we maximize our assets and minimize our liabilities? In what direction did we want the second half of our marriage to grow? What were our dreams—both individually and as a couple?

Up to this point, our marriage had been good—not perfect and not without struggles and daily challenges. For instance, Claudia tends to become quite intense at times, and how does Dave react? By not being serious and laughing things off. And Dave's best time is at night, while Claudia is the family early bird. We still struggle with who does what around the house, since neither of us are energized by housework. And we won't get into our struggle to eat nutritious meals on a regular basis.

Still, we classified our marriage as a growing marriage—that is, we are both committed to making our marriage better day by day. But we knew that if we wanted to experience positive growth in the second half of our marriage, we could not coast now. We needed to continue to courageously work on building for the future.

OUR PASSION FOR OUR MARRIAGE

The next day, over two bowls of clam chowder, we talked about our passion for our marriage and identified areas where we wanted to define specific goals for the autumn of our marriage. Our chronic back problems put physical fitness near the top of our list. We agreed to get back to our regular exercise routine. Other areas in which we set new goals were our love life and our relationship with our parents and adult children. We wanted to keep relationships with our sons and daughters-in-law healthy and reach a positive balance between caring and letting go.

We talked about ways we could grow together spiritually in our relationship with God. Also, we discussed financial goals and the need to seriously address retirement planning. Professionally, how could we narrow our focus and make the greatest impact in the productive years we still had before us? What about fun and leisure? For these areas too we needed to have specific goals.

OUR DESIRE IS TO FINISH WELL

On our last day, as we watched the splendor of the brilliant leaves venturing away from the safety of the aging trees and gently tumbling toward the earth, we talked of those years that would be the autumn and winter of our lives.

Our deepest desire is to finish well. In 2 Timothy 4:7, the apostle Paul speaks of finishing the race: "I have fought the good fight, I have finished the race, I have kept the faith." We asked ourselves a sobering question: "When we finish the race, what do we want our marriage to look like?" We actually made a list of things we hope will describe us when we've been married fifty-plus years:

We want to be best friends and close companions.

We want to have a positive outlook on life.

We want to have plans for the future, and as much as we don't like to think about one of us dying, we want to live a fulfilling life even if one of us is left alone without the other.

We want to continue to grow intellectually and be interesting people.

We want to enjoy our family while realizing we can't be the center of their lives.

As we talked about the future, we thought of older couples we knew who had "finished well." While some seemed to have happy marriages after fifty years together, there was one couple who were a living example of a godly marriage finishing well. Our list of what we wanted for our marriage described our friends and mentors Drs. David and Vera Mace.

MEET OUR MENTORS

For years, we had been influenced by the Maces' writings. The Maces initiated the marriage enrichment movement in Protestant churches, along with Father Calvo, who started Marriage Encounter (a weekend retreat to help couples learn how to better communicate with each other and grow closer in their marriage). From their experience as behavioral scientists, marriage counselors, and educators, the Maces realized that by the time those with troubled marriages seek help, it is often too late. So on their fortieth wedding anniversary, they started the Association for Couples in Marriage Enrichment, an international organization for the advancement of marriage enrichment.[2]

The Maces' goal was to work for better marriages, beginning with their own. As we came to know them personally in the early eighties, we could see they had been successful! We had just returned to the United States after living for a number of years in Europe and were delighted to realize that the Maces lived only three hours from us.

From time to time the Maces led training for marriage enrichment leaders, so we immediately signed up to participate.

We'll never forget that first evening when we met David and Vera. We arrived at the training conference in Black Mountain, North Carolina, with a little apprehension. As we sat at the Maces' table and ate dinner together, we immediately observed a twinkle in their eyes as they looked at each other. The spark in their relationship was contagious. As they talked with the group during the evening session, it was almost as if two were speaking as one. We were fascinated with their style of communication and how their marriage was a true partnership. Later that night, we both agreed that we had found a living model of what we wanted for our marriage.

Do you know such a couple? If so, you're halfway there! If not, let us encourage you to look around and find a couple who could be mentors for your marriage. Think about what you want your marriage to look like when you've been married for fifty or more years. How would you define "finishing well" for your marriage? Now is the time to invest in your marriage. Later you will reap the rewards. You may even become a mentor to younger couples.

BACK TO OUR FUTURE

While our week in New England was coming to a close, we had only begun to explore our future. But we had identified areas for growth and renewed our commitment to each other and to our marriage. We didn't have answers to all of our questions, but we were determined to search them out.

All too soon it was time to pack up the car and head back to Knoxville, but we left refreshed and with a new zeal and excitement for our marriage. Years later, after that lovely, reflective New England trip, we are still answering some of the questions we talked about that week. Our marriage goals are fluid and we keep changing them, but they help us face the future with courage and focus.

TAKE THE RISK

While driving home to our empty nest, we decided to risk forging a more intimate relationship for the coming years. Years afterward our marriage is still very much in process. Something is always in flux. Family dynamics change, situations change, and life is a continual adjustment. From our work with couples over the last few decades, we have observed that marriages are fluid. A marriage is either going forward or backward; standing still is not an option.

Are you willing to take the risk to grow together in your marriage so the second half is far better than the first half? It may involve making yourself more vulnerable to your spouse and disclosing yourself in a deeper way. Or it may involve rearranging your schedule, learning new skills, or changing some of your personal habits. But if you want to have a more personal and satisfying relationship with your spouse for the second half of marriage, we encourage you to take this challenge seriously.

Are you willing to create a relationship that preserves the best from the first half of your marriage but at the same time offers you the freedom to adapt and grow in new ways? The ability to make such a creative choice is one of the joys of becoming middle-aged! Reaching middle age comes with certain privileges and credentials. We who are in this stage of life are more assertive. We know better who we are, what we want, and how to get it. We should have better judgment and possibly even more financial resources to translate our desires into deeds than we did in the earlier years of our marriage. Perhaps, like us, you are discovering that maturity does have it privileges.

WHERE ARE YOU?

Where are you in your marriage journey? Are you in the middle of those turbulent adolescent years? Did you pick this book up to dream about the empty nest and to look for light at the end of the tunnel? Let us encourage you. You can begin today to prepare for those coming years. Much that you can do now will insure that the second half of your marriage will be the better half.

Perhaps you are just beginning the process of emptying your nest, and you're looking for some help in getting off on the right foot with this new relationship built for two. We want to guide you through the process of reinventing your marriage. We want to help you hold on to the best from the first half and discover new and exciting ways to build an enriched marriage for the second half.

Or maybe you're well into the second half of your marriage. Things aren't going so well, and you're looking for hope. There is hope! James Peterson, who at the University of Southern California headed up a major study on aging for the American Association of Retired Persons (AARP), said that one of the most exciting things he discovered is that old people can change their behavior up to the day of their death![3] It is never too early or too late to make changes for the better to ensure marital success. So if you feel you're already set in your ways and cannot change, you're wrong. You can change and improve your marriage, for as long as you both shall live!

OUR INVITATION

Won't you join us as fellow sojourners? We invite you to travel with us through this journey. In the following pages, we will share with you the progress we have made. Our own personal search led us to conduct a national survey on the second half of marriage, and from our survey results, we will give you specific suggestions that can help you make the rest of your marriage the best.

We'll share with you what is working for us and for other couples—and we'll help you avoid some of the things that don't work—so you can revitalize your marriage. Our desire for you as you read through the following pages is that you too will renew your zest for your partner and will look to the future with hope and anticipation of all that is in store for you in the second half of your marriage. It's now your turn to look closer at your own marriage!

Surveying the Second Half
of Marriage

———— ✑ ————

It takes guts to stay married. . . . There will be many crises between the wedding day and the golden anniversary, and the people who make it are heroes.

—Howard Whiteman[1]

After returning from our refreshing New England empty-nest trip filled with happy memories, we began our search for resources that would help us in the second half of our marriage. We were amazed to discover how few resources mentioned life after forty. Those that did usually dealt with recovery and serious issues.

We found materials on divorce recovery, midlife crisis (especially for males), relating to adult children, and we even found a number of books on retirement planning. But how to have a healthy, enriched marriage in midlife and beyond? Information was conspicuously absent!

When we talked to people about the second half of marriage, we discovered that most hadn't even thought about it. Our friends Lou and Katy were married several years before they had children, and while they are close to fifty, they still have three teenagers at home. We asked Katy what she was looking forward to in the next twenty-five years of her marriage.

"The next twenty-five years?" Katy replied. "I just want to get through today."

When we questioned Lou, he said, "We're looking forward to serving God together."

While this is a noble goal, his comment seemed a little vague. How would you answer the question? What are your dreams and hopes for the next twenty-five years of your marriage? What do you think about when you hear the term "the second half of marriage"?

THE SECOND HALF OF MARRIAGE

Are you in the second half of marriage? Check out these symptoms:

You have teenagers who will soon leave the nest.

Your own parents are aging.

You were recently invited to a twenty-fifth high school reunion.

You exercise more and burn fewer calories doing it.

You just received an invitation to join AARP.

By the time you get your spouse's attention, you've forgotten what you were going to say.

If you identify with these symptoms, you are in or are approaching the second half of marriage. The first half of marriage involved launching your union and surviving the active parenting years. Did you, like us, think those children would be around forever? Of course there are a number of couples, like Lou and Katy, who waited until later to start their family and are still parenting in their forties and fifties. For them, menopause and the adolescent years may hit simultaneously, making the challenge in the second half of marriage even greater!

With the birthing of the second half of marriage, couples enter an uncharted course where mentors are few and far between. In the past, people did not live as long as they do today. Now you may live a healthy, productive life into your eighties or even your nineties! Increased longevity has many implications for your marriage. A second-half marriage as long or longer than the first half provides the opportunity to build a closer friendship, to set new goals, to travel and pursue new interests and hobbies, to begin a new profession, to influence your adult children and grandchildren, and to continue to make an impact on this world in one way or another. The second half can be the best time of life! But marriage at this stage comes with challenges.

THE MIDLIFE MARRIAGE CRISIS

The transition into the second half of marriage is a crisis time for many couples. The current trend is alarming: long-term marriages are breaking up in record numbers. According to the National Center of Health Statistics, although divorce in the United States generally declined from 1981 to 1991, divorce among couples married thirty years or more showed a sharp increase. Overall, divorce went down 1.4 percent during the decade, while divorce in the thirty-years-plus marriages increased 16 percent.[2]

Why the jump in divorces for this age group? Could it be that as people begin to realize they are going to live longer, they don't want to spend the rest of their life in an unhappy and unfulfilled marriage? One husband, married twenty-five years, commented, "We never had a very close relationship, but the kids kept us together—they were our connecting point. When they left home, it was just the two of us, with no buffers. We had nothing in common and decided it was crazy to waste the rest of our lives. So we divorced."

While many long-term marriages avoid divorce, other second-half issues can produce much stress. The children grow up and leave home, our parents age and die, we may add a few pounds and more bulges, and we may have less energy and move slower. Just as we become more aware of the aging process, life gets complicated—one career may be winding down while the other spouse's career is taking off. We begin to realize how fast life goes by and that if we are going to make changes, we'd better hurry, because we don't have a lot of time left. No wonder midlife couples experience new levels of stress!

We decided to take the initiative. How could we help meet the challenges facing midlife marriages? We have always been careful to guard our own marriage. How could we help others who also wanted to protect their midlife marriage and to promote growth in it? To help answer this question, we put together a survey to enable us to better understand the dynamics of long-term marriages and find answers to the difficult questions facing all midlife marriages.

HOW WE DEVELOPED OUR SURVEY

Over the years, we have talked to people around the world and asked them about their marriages and families. For instance, last year while on a special assignment with the United Nations in Vienna, Austria, we interviewed people from numerous countries. As people told us about their families and marriages, we asked them what areas were problematic and what areas were the most satisfying.

The patterns we saw in our personal interviews led us to develop a formal written survey, which we mailed to 5000 people. We received more than 500 written responses. We also recorded answers from others with whom we conducted personal interviews. In the coming pages, we will share our discoveries from that survey.

We wanted to measure the degree of satisfaction in long-term marriages and to identify the major issues facing midlife marriages. We chose twenty different categories to explore and designed a simple survey to measure satisfaction in each of these areas. Additional essay questions probed the best aspects of the participants' marriages, what caused them stress, what they feared most about the future, and what they looked forward to. We also asked for empty nest tips. Some participants wrote pages. Others photocopied our survey and passed it on to friends, Sunday school classes, and other small groups. We received mailed responses from all over the United States—even some from Europe. Even as we complete this book, we are still receiving responses. This indicates great interest today in how marriages can work in the second half.

While this was not a random survey (the participants were generally of the Christian faith), we believe that our results reflect our culture today, especially when we acknowledge that the divorce rate is basically the same for secular and religious groups. However, it is important to note that most of our survey participants were in long-term marriages (or in second marriages they hope will be long-term), indicating a high degree of commitment that may not exist in the population at large.

Comments from those who participated in our survey are sprinkled throughout this book. To protect their privacy, we only indicate if the comment is from a husband or wife, and the number of years the person has been married. To begin your own marriage evaluation, we invite you to answer our survey questions.

SURVEYING YOUR MARRIAGE

The surveys at the end of this chapter list twenty different categories. Check your level of satisfaction as it relates to your marriage. Then reflect on the best aspects of your marriage, what causes you stress, what you fear most about the future, and what you are looking forward to. Use this exercise as a way to evaluate where you are in your marriage. (Extra copies are available at the end of the book.)

Note: Change and growth starts with one heart. If you are reading this book alone, growth in your marriage can start with you. You can do this exercise on your own by first filling it out for yourself. Then go through it again and fill it out the way you think your spouse would rate each area. Or you can benefit from this survey as a couple. From time to time we enjoy filling out the questions individually and then comparing our answers and discussing them. It reveals little areas we still need to work on. For instance, the last time we did this, Claudia only registered a six in satisfaction under household responsibilities, while Dave recorded a perfect ten. Guess who needs to take out more trash and assume more responsibility?

WHAT YOUR SURVEY REVEALED

Did you find our survey a challenging experience? If your spouse also participated, were your ratings similar? Were you surprised?

One word of caution: If your mate rated an area lower than you did, it could mean he or she simply has higher expectations in that area. A high rating can also mean low expectations. The degree you rated the different categories is not as significant as your willingness to discuss them with your spouse and to talk about where you want to be in the future. (After completing this book, you may want to retake the survey and check progress made. Extra surveys are in the appendix on page 217.) Also, if you identified areas for improvement, as you go through this book you will have the opportunity to work on many of them.

Now compare your ratings with the other participants'.

GENERAL SURVEY RESULTS

As we compiled and tabulated responses, we began to see that successful second-half marriages have several commonalities. We were encouraged as we realized that marital satisfaction tends to rise after the children grow up and leave home. However, the lowest time of martial satisfaction, as indicated by our survey, is when adolescent children are present. Consider the following chart:

Response to Questionnaire Answers out of 10	1= very unsatisfied		10= very satisfied	
Aspects of Marriage	Under 40	40-49	50-59	Over 60
Financial	5.96	6.58	7.24	8.54
Companionship	7.82	7.54	8.00	9.25
Spiritual Growth	6.36	6.94	7.77	8.65
Mutual Activities	6.43	6.70	7.24	8.49
Individual Activities	7.01	7.29	7.75	8.33
Communication	6.57	6.68	7.16	7.69
My Health	5.77	6.39	6.71	7.65
Mate's Health	6.11	6.91	6.85	7.71
Ministry	6.68	6.82	7.05	7.48
Friends & Family	7.07	7.17	7.51	8.48
Community	6.31	6.12	6.44	7.39
Romance	6.33	6.60	6.95	8.20
Household Resp.	6.58	6.97	7.78	8.32
Conflict Resolution	6.42	6.32	6.88	8.29
Sex	6.97	7.12	7.24	8.14
Education	6.94	7.16	7.63	8.27
Relationship/Children	7.66	7.31	8.04	8.68
Relationship/Grandchildren	low data	low data	6.18	9.10
Retirement	5.69	5.95	6.58	8.44
Relation/Aging Parents	7.33	6.34	7.14	8.73

BEST, WORST, FEARS, AND DREAMS

Let's look at the four essay questions. For each, we've summarized the answers we received, and then listed some typical comments.

What Are the Best Aspects of Your Marriage?

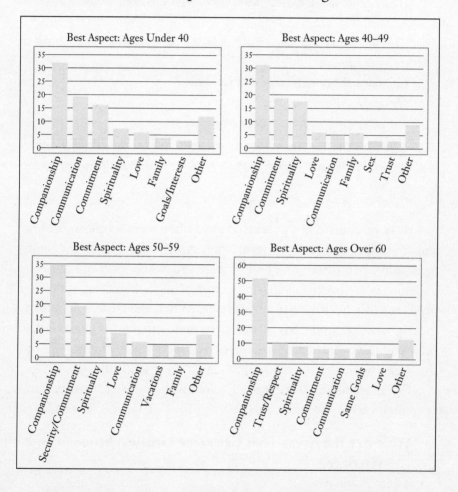

"Our friendship and the ability to work together on common goals."
"Strong communication skills, and we build each other up constantly."
"We are each other's best friend and really enjoy being together."
"My husband is my best friend, my confidant, my lover."
"Spiritual commitment and commitment to each other."

"Companionship and sexual fulfillment."

"Mutual commitment and faith in God."

"Our friendship, which we both treasure."

"We love each other and are best friends who inspire each other and stand together through the difficult times."

"We like each other, we let each other be ourselves, and we work together well."

"The support we give to each other during the good times and the not so good times."

"Commitment to each other and to Christ."

"Humor, love, worship, sex."

"Laughter and the fun we have together."

"Commitment to work to improve our marriage; commitment to God."

"Solid love and determination to make it work through the good and the bad."

"There is never a dull moment."

By far, the answers we received most often were "companionship" and "friendship." As the age levels increased, so did the answer "companionship." In the second half of marriage, when most of the hectic parenting years are history, having a strong couple-friendship is the best predictor of a healthy, happy marriage. When the answer "companionship" and/or "best friends" was given on the first essay question, the ratings of the twenty categories on chart 1 were usually higher. For us, this is an encouragement to keep building our friendship!

Other frequent answers were "commitment," "spirituality," and "communication."

What Are the Areas That Cause the Greatest Stress in Your Marriage?

"Talking about our budget and retirement plans."

"Being unwilling to forgive causes extreme pain."

"Our lack of communication."

"Definitely finances—we aren't broke, just have different and conflicting attitudes toward money."

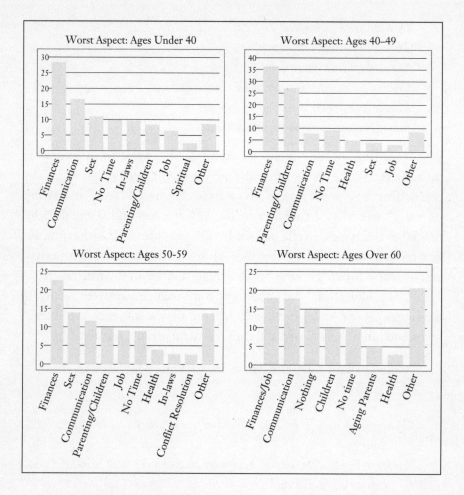

"Dealing with extended family."

"Our teenage children."

"Lack of spontaneity and romance."

"Money, sex, and time management."

"Disciplining our children."

"Relationships with our grown children."

"Money, money, and money."

"Finances, stepchildren, and sex."

"Time pressures—I feel we're out of control."

"Differences in our spiritual growth and beliefs."

"Lack of respect."

"Dealing with ex-spouses."
"Trying to control each other."
"Sex and conflict resolution."
"Cranky kids and the difference in our sex drive."
"Money and anger."
"Inability to discuss and resolve conflicts."

According to our survey, the number one stress in marriages is financial stress. But as the age levels increased, the percentage who indicated "finances" went down. Many times "money," "sex," and "time pressure" were listed together as the key stresses and seemed to be related to the typical hectic pace of life that couples face as they transition into the second half of marriage. However, 10 percent of those sixty and over still listed "no time" as the greatest stress in their marriage.

"Communication" and "children" were frequent answers. Many of the couples in our survey had children in the adolescent years. We already mentioned that this is a stressful time for the marriage relationship.

What Do You Fear the Most about Your Marriage in the Future?

"That one of us will become a burden to the other due to physical disabilities."
"Unforeseen changes, like ill health, that will force us to become dependent on our children."
"Lack of mutual enjoyment apart from child-oriented and family things."
"Divorce."
"That we won't earn enough money to live in a comfortable fashion."
"Having nothing in common."
"That our marriage will get worse."
"More financial trouble and possibly divorce."
"That my marriage will remain this way forever."
"That in the empty nest we will just coexist."
"Our children growing up and leaving home."
"We will go our separate ways because our priorities are so different."
"Loosing my mate."

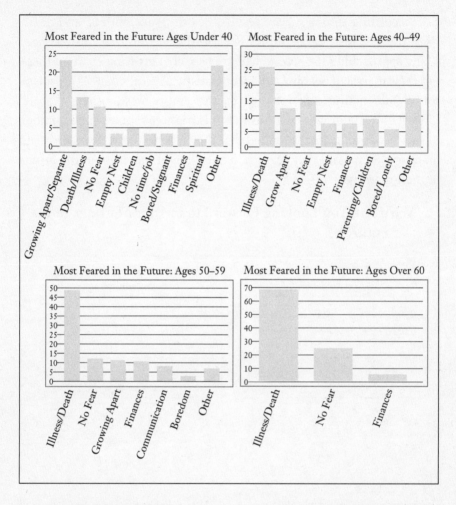

Most Feared in the Future: Ages Under 40

Most Feared in the Future: Ages 40–49

Most Feared in the Future: Ages 50–59

Most Feared in the Future: Ages Over 60

"No time for each other or ourselves as we care for aging parents and deal with teenagers and young adults."

"The loss of our children and growing apart."

"Apathy, boredom."

"Emotional separation because of unresolved conflicts."

"Having the children leave home and we not having anything in common."

"That my mate would die before me."

"That he will find someone slimmer, prettier, and more exciting than I am and have an affair or leave."

According to our survey results, health issues, illness, and death were the greatest fears couples have in the second half of marriage. Many approaching the second half are fearful of growing apart and seeing their marriage become a divorce statistic. Again, finances are a factor. While many look forward to the empty nest, others fear it. Uncertainty about what the future holds frightens some, but a number of survey participants responded that they had no future fears for their marriage. Some said they really had not thought much about the future of their marriage.

What Are You Looking Forward to in Your Marriage in the Future?

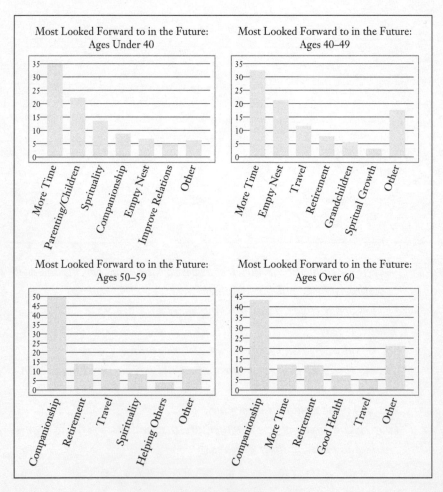

"Having a closer relationship."
"Growing closer to each other."
"Having less conflict with the children gone."
"Having more time together in the empty nest."
"Growing old with my lifetime friend and companion."
"More time for personal and mutual growth as the children leave."
"Growing together spiritually."
"Doing more fun things as time and money allow."
"Not being so tired when it comes to making time for intimacy and sex."
"Just surviving!"
"More time and money to do things together."
"Nothing."
"Growing old and celebrating our fiftieth together."
"To love again."
"More together time and traveling."
"A miracle."
"I'm praying that things will change."
"To travel and camp with my husband."
"Having our fifteen-year-old graduate and leave for college, so we will have the house to ourselves and more freedom and intimacy in our love life."
"Getting out of debt."
"Increased financial security, which will enable us to travel together."
"Years of companionship."
"Somehow rebuilding our marriage."

Again, companionship rated as the number one thing spouses are looking forward to! Even some who indicated they had little communication and much conflict had high hopes and desires to be best friends in the empty nest! As the age level increased, companionship as an important desire and goal increased.

Spouses also look forward to the empty nest. They look forward to traveling together and to retirement. Children and grandchildren were listed, but not as often as one might think. Again we observed that the key to healthy long-term marriages is the ability to become best friends and close companions! How would you rate your friendship with your mate? If that aspect of your marriage needs a little work, it's a challenge worth considering.

CHALLENGING YOUR MARRIAGE FOR THE SECOND HALF

From our survey, we discovered that for couples who hang together through the midlife transition, marital satisfaction begins to rise again and stays that way—if couples risk growing in their relationship. The second half of marriage gives you the opportunity to reinvent your marriage, to make midcourse adjustments, and to reconnect with one another in a more meaningful way. Healthy long-term marriages have staying power, because they are held together from within. Competent couples invest time and energy in building and maintaining a positive relationship with each other.

From our work in marriage enrichment over the years, and based on our survey, we believe that the following eight challenges describe the areas in which couples with healthy long-term marriages are investing their energies. We are convinced that if you work on these eight challenges, your marriage will be enriched. If you do not surmount these challenges, your marriage will not be as fulfilling as it could be.

The Eight Marital Challenges for the Second Half of Marriage

1. Let go of past marital disappointments, forgive each other, and commit to making the rest of your marriage the best. Are you willing to let go of unmet expectations and unrealistic dreams? What about that missed promotion—for either you or your spouse? Can you give up your dream for a condo on the ski slope? Or maybe you are realizing that your kid is never going to be a Rhodes scholar or professional baseball player. Can you accept those extra pounds? Those gray hairs—or lack of hair? Your mate's little irritating habits don't seem to be disappearing—can you accept them?

Giving up lost dreams and dealing with each other's imperfections is a positive step toward forgiving past hurts and moving on in your marriage. Holding on to marital grudges and disappointments will only prevent you from moving on in your relationship and developing a new, more loving marriage.

2. Create a marriage that is partner-focused rather than child-focused. Too often when the children leave the nest, couples move from a child-focused marriage to an activity-focused marriage. Community or church activities may now take up the time and energy formerly devoted to children. Unfortunately, these activities may still be buffers to a mutual, partnership marriage. How can you make the transition to a partner-focused relationship?

In the second half of marriage, the dynamics of the relationship change. Roles and functions that previously worked are no longer relevant. Without children as distractions, you have the opportunity to refocus and redefine your marriage. Marriage in the second half can be more personal and more fulfilling as you focus on the couple relationship and not on children.

3. Maintain an effective communication system that allows you to express your deepest feelings, joys, and concerns. What can you do when the communication patterns that seemed to work during the first half of marriage are found to be inadequate and lacking for the second half? With the children absent, there are more spaces of silence; there is less to say to each other. You may ask yourself, *We made it this far—why is it now so difficult to have a really personal conversation?*

When we begin to talk about really personal matters, it's easy to feel threatened. Midlife is a time when it is vitally important to develop interpersonal competence—the ability to converse on a personal level by sharing your deepest feelings, joys, and concerns. Successful couples are able to find a proper balance between intimacy and autonomy, and this is critical for healthy relationships in the second half of marriage.

4. Use anger and conflict in a creative way to build your relationship. Love and anger can both be used to build your marriage, but you must process your anger in an appropriate way and develop a proper balance that allows you to express your concerns in the context of a loving relationship. A healthy marriage is a safe place to resolve honest conflict and process anger. The reason this challenge is so critical to long-term marriages is that in most conflict situations, it isn't the facts that are the real problem, it's the strong negative (or even angry) feelings we harbor. Once those feelings are dealt with, it's simple to move on and work at resolving the conflict.

5. *Build a deeper friendship and enjoy your spouse.* At this stage of marriage, we can deepen our friendship and become close companions. One advantage of a long-term marriage is being more familiar and comfortable with each other. We know we aren't perfect, so we can relax and enjoy each other.

What are you doing to build your friendship with your spouse? Are you taking care of your health and pacing yourself for the second half? What are you doing to stretch your boundaries and prevent boredom? The second half of marriage is a great time to develop as "couple friends." How can we put more fun in our marriage and use humor to diminish the effects of an already too serious world? Friendship and fun in marriage—especially in the second half—is serious business!

6. *Renew romance and restore a pleasurable sexual relationship.* Many people assume that as people grow older, they loose interest in sex. Research shows otherwise. Amazingly, our survey results suggest that sexual satisfaction increases rather than decreases with number of years married. As we enter the second half of marriage, it is important for us to protect our privacy, cherish our love relationship, and renew romance, while acknowledging the inevitable changes in our bodies. The quality of our love life is not so much a matter of performance as it is a function of the quality of our relationship.

7. *Adjust to changing roles with aging parents and adult children.* Just as you need to release your children into adulthood, you need to reconnect with them on an adult level. At the same time, you need to balance relationships with your own parents. If your parents did not successfully meet this challenge in their marriage, it may be more difficult for you. Whatever your situation, the relationship with your elderly parents and your adult children definitely has an effect on your marriage. Realizing and accepting what is realistic in your own family relation-

ships is so important. You can't go back and change your past family history, but what you do in the future is your choice and decision. You can choose to forge better relationships with those loved ones on both sides of the generational seesaw.

8. Evaluate where you are on your spiritual pilgrimage, grow closer to each other and to God, and together serve others. Our faith in God and his banner of love over our marriage should make a difference in the quality of our marriage—especially in the second half. The relationship of the husband and the wife to God is tested and validated in their relationship to each other. The closeness we have when we pray together is a closeness we can achieve in no other way. Let us challenge you to evaluate where you are on your own spiritual pilgrimage and to seek to grow closer spiritually to each other and to God. To meet this challenge, first you must be on a spiritual journey, your journey must have your attention, and your journey must be a priority. Also important to your marriage is a commitment to serve others and pass along the wisdom you have gained. This commitment is a natural outgrowth of love for God.

THE MARRIAGE JOURNEY

Marital success comes through daily struggles. Marriage is made up of the daily grind—the little things like making unselfish choices and forgiving each other help to build a healthy marriage. Little steps, if taken in good faith, can turn the tide. But it helps to have a plan. So let's take a deeper look at each second-half challenge, with the hope of inspiring you to come up with your own plan!

Our desire for you as you read through the following pages is that you will gain new insights and knowledge that will motivate you to make the rest of your marriage the best. The choice is yours.

❧

MARRIAGE BUILDER

Reflecting On My Marriage

Look through the following reflective questions about your marriage. Choose several to discuss with your spouse.

1. In what areas do we need adjustments for this time of transition (for example, roles, functions, how we handle anger)?

2. What are our dreams (individually and as a couple)?

3. What do I want our marriage to look like when we come to the end of the race?

4. Who are (or could be) our marriage mentors?

5. What is my passion? Do we have a "couple passion"?

6. What are our financial goals? Retirement plans?

7. What am I doing for my health and physical fitness?

8. What do we do for fun and leisure?

MARRIAGE BUILDER

Surveying the Second Half of Marriage

Check your level of satisfaction in the following general categories as they relate to your marriage:

Areas of satisfaction or dissatisfaction:

	very dissatisfied			neither				very satisfied		
	1	2	3	4	5	6	7	8	9	10
Financial management	—	—	—	—	—	—	—	—	—	—
Companionship	—	—	—	—	—	—	—	—	—	—
Spiritual growth and commitment	—	—	—	—	—	—	—	—	—	—
Mutual activities	—	—	—	—	—	—	—	—	—	—
Individual activities	—	—	—	—	—	—	—	—	—	—
Communication with mate	—	—	—	—	—	—	—	—	—	—
My health and physical fitness	—	—	—	—	—	—	—	—	—	—
Mate's health and physical fitness	—	—	—	—	—	—	—	—	—	—
Ministry activities	—	—	—	—	—	—	—	—	—	—
Friends and extended family	—	—	—	—	—	—	—	—	—	—
Community service	—	—	—	—	—	—	—	—	—	—
Romance and intimacy	—	—	—	—	—	—	—	—	—	—
Household responsibilities	—	—	—	—	—	—	—	—	—	—
Conflict resolution	—	—	—	—	—	—	—	—	—	—
Sexual fulfillment	—	—	—	—	—	—	—	—	—	—
Education and career development	—	—	—	—	—	—	—	—	—	—
Relationship with children	—	—	—	—	—	—	—	—	—	—
Relationship with grandchildren	—	—	—	—	—	—	—	—	—	—
Retirement plan	—	—	—	—	—	—	—	—	—	—
Relationship with aging parents	—	—	—	—	—	—	—	—	—	—

1. What are the best aspects of your marriage?

2. What are the areas that cause the greatest stress in your marriage?

3. What do you fear the most about your marriage in the future?

4. What are you looking forward to in your marriage in the future?

MARRIAGE BUILDER

Surveying the Second Half of Marriage

Check your level of satisfaction in the following general categories as they relate to your marriage:

Areas of satisfaction or dissatisfaction:

	very dissatisfied			neither			very satisfied		
	1	2	3	4	5	6	7	8	9	10
Financial management	__	__	__	__	__	__	__	__	__	__
Companionship	__	__	__	__	__	__	__	__	__	__
Spiritual growth and commitment	__	__	__	__	__	__	__	__	__	__
Mutual activities	__	__	__	__	__	__	__	__	__	__
Individual activities	__	__	__	__	__	__	__	__	__	__
Communication with mate	__	__	__	__	__	__	__	__	__	__
My health and physical fitness	__	__	__	__	__	__	__	__	__	__
Mate's health and physical fitness	__	__	__	__	__	__	__	__	__	__
Ministry activities	__	__	__	__	__	__	__	__	__	__
Friends and extended family	__	__	__	__	__	__	__	__	__	__
Community service	__	__	__	__	__	__	__	__	__	__
Romance and intimacy	__	__	__	__	__	__	__	__	__	__
Household responsibilities	__	__	__	__	__	__	__	__	__	__
Conflict resolution	__	__	__	__	__	__	__	__	__	__
Sexual fulfillment	__	__	__	__	__	__	__	__	__	__
Education and career development	__	__	__	__	__	__	__	__	__	__
Relationship with children	__	__	__	__	__	__	__	__	__	__
Relationship with grandchildren	__	__	__	__	__	__	__	__	__	__
Retirement plan	__	__	__	__	__	__	__	__	__	__
Relationship with aging parents	__	__	__	__	__	__	__	__	__	__

1. What are the best aspects of your marriage?

2. What are the areas that cause the greatest stress in your marriage?

3. What do you fear the most about your marriage in the future?

4. What are you looking forward to in your marriage in the future?

PART TWO

❧

Facing Eight Midlife Marital Challenges

———— ❧ ————

He is the half part of a blessed man,
Left to be finished by such as she;
And she a fair divided excellence,
Whose fullness of perfection lies in him.

—Shakespeare

Challenge One

❧

*Let Go of Past Marital Disappointments,
Forgive Each Other, and Commit to Making
the Rest of Your Marriage the Best*

---

*After twenty years of marriage, I finally realized my husband
will never be home at five p.m. While this is disappointing to me,
I simply had to let that expectation go.*

—wife married for twenty-five years

*So we never will build our dream house or be able to retire at fifty-
five. We still have each other, and for us that's what is important.*

—husband married for thirty-two years

*During times of testing and disappointments, we kept working
on our relationship. We learned how to forgive each other and
how to work things out. We are committed to our marriage
and we never give up. That's our secret.*

—wife married for forty-seven years

*Even at times when love was questioned, commitment wasn't!
We chose to forgive each other, and the result is a marriage
of total trust, faith, and of an ever deepening love and
appreciation for my partner.*

—wife married for twenty-five years

The recipe for success in marriage is effort plus insight.

—David and Vera Mace[1]

We are both list makers. Dave has even been known to make lists after the fact—just so he can mark things off and feel good about his accomplishments. Claudia makes lists and then forgets where she put them. But when we returned home after our New England empty-nest trip, we made a list that was quite different from the run-of-the-mill "to do" lists.

We made a list of things we will never do or change. For us it was an important step in letting go of unrealistic dreams and expectations and in getting on with our future. We had to admit to each other that some things just weren't going to change. Things we had hoped to do by this stage of life were not going to happen; we couldn't realistically do all those things we had planned to do when the children grew up.

Our list included things like: we will never be a family unit of five again; we will never have a daughter (however, we think our grand-daughter, Sophie, more than compensates for this!); our backs will never be completely healthy again; and we can never go long periods without exercise and not experience pain (it hurts to even think about it!).

We will never build a mountain cabin with three teenage boys. We will never be competitive in tennis. Claudia, the competitive one, will never consistently beat Dave and never give up wanting to. And our last run down a black-diamond ski slope is history (or *we* soon would be!). Sadly, we admit we will probably never get our office really organized. Dave will just have to tolerate Claudia's creative filing system. Claudia will have to give Dave the grace to sneak ice cream late at night when we are both trying to diet, and we will probably never declutter our house. Claudia will probably never wear size eight again; Dave will never grow more hair.

DEALING WITH UNMET EXPECTATIONS AND LOST DREAMS

As the years pass, our "we'll never do" list gets longer. This past summer in Europe, we added: "We will never ride across the Swiss Alps on a motorcycle." And we finally went through our closets and gave away those clothes that still don't fit and that we'll never wear!

Some things will not change, and that includes some of our little irritations—like one of us forgetting to turn the thermostat down and we both wake up in the middle of the night in a hot sweat, or one of us forgetting to squeeze the toothpaste from the bottom of the tube. Actually, marriage reminds us of a spiral staircase. You go around in circles and keep running into the same issues time and time again. Circumstances may be a little different and your perspective may change, but every marriage has stumbling blocks that keep tripping you up and slowing you down. And these little issues, when not dealt with, lead to discouragement and disappointment again and again. When the children grow up and leave home, these little irritations often become glaring and obvious.

When a long-term marriage crumbles, most of the time it isn't because of a major crisis or a one-time event. More likely, it's the result of little issues that have built up over the years until they threaten the very foundation of the marriage. We keep hoping that our mate will shape up and change, but it just doesn't happen.

Everyone thought Brad and Tina had the ideal marriage. No one knew they were really "divorced-marrieds." They lived under the same roof, but each lived a separate life. They even had separate bedrooms. How did this happen? It started with a little irritation that grew into a big deal. When they were first married, Brad hogged the covers, and Tina would wake up shivering in the middle of the night, with no blanket—Brad had the whole blanket tucked neatly under him. Nightly she struggled to recover her share of the blanket. Night after night the scenario repeated itself. Finally this irritation escalated to the point of their choosing separate bedrooms.

We may gasp and say, "We'd never have separate bedrooms!" Still, we let each other down in other ways. Perhaps your mate is no longer the petite size six you married; she always gave lip service to getting in shape, but her more than fifteen years as a size twelve now suggest that you're only going to see your petite wife in photographs. Or maybe your mate has never realized his potential as a conversationalist. When you were in college together, you saw a glimmer of deep thoughts waiting to be expressed, but somewhere along the line he just stopped talking.

Stop for a moment and think back to those days long ago when you met and fell in love. Do you remember the energy, excitement, and sheer enthusiasm you had for each other? Do you remember thinking that you had met your ideal counterpart? Then you got married and rode off into the sunset with your Prince or Princess Charming, only to discover he or she had some irritating habits and wasn't quite as charming as you thought. The stars in your eyes faded enough for you to see each other's idiosyncrasies and faults.

Unfortunately, these irritations can do more than just irritate. When we fail to deal with these irritations, either by changing or accepting them, intimacy is redefined and emotional distance increases.

It's easy to find a low-intimacy comfort level, and sometimes— without your realizing what is happening—your marriage relationship takes a backseat to your family, profession, church, and community. Interpersonal disappointments are still there, but they are buried under the surface of a hectic family life. Then the children begin leaving home, and you realize that not only is your partner a far cry from Prince Charming, he doesn't even look like a prince; you begin to realize that your dreams for your marriage didn't materialize. You're not sure what the future may hold, but you're disappointed with where you are right now.

Before you can regroup and reignite your relationship, you must deal with your own disappointments, let go of past hurts and lost dreams.

MAKE YOUR OWN "I'LL NEVER DO" LIST

You may want to make your own "I'll never do" list. To look realistically at your own relationship and situation will help you surmount the first part of this initial challenge for the second half of your marriage: to let go of past marital disappointments, to accept your spouse with his or her faults, realizing that when you married, it was a package deal!

When we come to the place of really accepting each other and realizing we will not reform our mate, the next logical step is to be willing to forgive our imperfect partner.

FORGIVENESS IS DIVINE

Forgiveness is a key element in healthy long-term marriages. Forgiveness is the oil that lubricates a love relationship, and it's an oil we need daily. Forgiveness is not a one-time event; it's an attitude of wanting to partner with your spouse in spite of his or her imperfections and irritations.

Our Marriage Alive seminar is a marriage enrichment workshop geared for couples who basically have stable marriages but want to make them better. Occasionally, however, we will have a group whose marital issues need much more time to work out. On a recent trip to Europe, we had the opportunity to lead several seminars; one stands out in our minds as particularly challenging. We were all set for a fun and enriching experience, when we began to meet some of the couples who were attending. We instantly realized our predicament. While some of the couples had growing marriages, others were just barely hanging on.

One key session dealt with understanding and accepting each other and being willing to forgive each other. While we kept emphasizing the importance of forgiveness, some of the participants just didn't get it. One wife asked us in sheer frustration, "How long does it take to forgive your mate?"

Our answer was, "As long as it takes!"

"But," she answered back, "I forgive him, and then the same thing comes up again and again!"

We reminded her that long-standing problems take time to resolve. You can't solve in one day what took years to create. However, there are steps that can be taken.

TWO-STEP FORGIVENESS

We suggested two important steps:

1. Decide to forgive.
2. Don't put a limit on forgiveness.

Our friend Jennifer took both steps. For years she has been the foundation of her rocky marriage. If her marriage to Frank were based on each giving their own fifty percent, she would have bailed out years ago. All who know Frank wonder how he could be married to such a wonderful person. Frank is hardworking, domineering, and demanding. He would not be the easiest person to live with. Most people we know would have thrown in the towel, but not Jennifer. Now well into the second half of her marriage, Jennifer discussed that relationship with us, and we were amazed at what she told us: "My marriage is my dearest treasure. Frank has become my best friend. We are closer than we have ever been."

"How did you do it?" we asked her. "How did you get to the point where the second half of your marriage is better than the first?"

"I never put a limit on forgiveness," she said. "And I continually tried to do my part the very best I could. I can't control Frank, but I can control me. I can't do anything about his actions, but I can control mine. I had to stop asking myself, *What do I deserve in this situation?* Instead, I ask, *What can I give in this situation?* I can only change one person's actions, and that person is me.

"It's amazing, though, over the years as I've worked on changing me, how Frank has modified his behavior as well. He's actually spending less time at work and more time with me. We took up golf, so that's something else we can do together.

"I've always tried to grab the best from the past and focus on the future. Because my marriage is so precious to me, I haven't been willing to throw it away because 'I'm right' in a situation and he is wrong. Also, a long time ago I realized it's much easier to put things back together in the framework of a marriage, so I never considered divorce."

Decide to Forgive

Is there something right now that disappoints you about your mate or your relationship? Grievances can range in intensity from habitually leaving the TV on to having illicit affairs. No matter where your disappointments and hurts fall on the continuum, you must decide to forgive your spouse and move beyond these grievances before you can work on developing an exuberant, growing marriage in the second half. Keep in mind that some issues may necessitate the help of a professional counselor or pastor—please seek out this help if you just can't find a way to let go of your anger and pain.

If, however, your issues lie more toward your mate not maintaining the figure you fell in love with or not helping with the dishes after dinner, it's time to let go and move on. Here's the process we suggest to move you toward forgiveness:

Identify grievances. OK, here's the list you may have rattled off in your head, or to your spouse, a thousand times. Now write it down! You won't show this list to your mate (you'll burn it or bury it when you're through), but you need to articulate to yourself once and for all every little thing that continually crops up in your relationship. So do it now!

Evaluate grievances. Now take this list and evaluate which issues can be easily forgiven and forgotten (like leaving tissues in the kitchen sink), which issues need some special closure because they still cause you some pain (your mate's refusal to take up your favorite hobby), which issues need to be discussed because you're still not sure it's time to let them go (people can always loose a few pounds, right?), and which issues will take a serious effort on your part, perhaps even professional intervention, to overcome (affairs, no lovemaking, abusive communication patterns).

Let's note here that although all bad habits can be changed and it is never too late to teach an old dog new tricks, you can't change your mate; you can only change your responses to your mate.

Decide to forgive. For each item on your list, ask yourself if you are willing to forgive your mate and let go of this issue between you. Remember, forgiveness begins with a simple decision, a simple act of the will. We are to forgive as God has forgiven us. It is not dependent upon our spouse asking for our forgiveness or even acknowledging he or she has done anything wrong.

Let go. With your categorized list, decide on an appropriate send-off for the easily forgiven and forgotten irritations. Perhaps setting the list on fire and dropping it into the toilet. Or if appropriate, consider wrapping the list in a box and giving it to your mate with a note saying, "I promise to never be bothered by these, your previously incredibly irritating but now lovable idiosyncratic behaviors. This is my gift to you for the second half of our marriage."

For the issues that still cause you some pain, like your mate never joining you in a particular sport, hobby, or other activity, make a plan on how to fill this need in your life without your mate. If golf is an important part of your life but your mate will never participate, find someone else to be your partner in this aspect of your life, and let go of the disappointment that your mate will never fill this role. We can't be everything to all people, most especially to our mate.

Now to the issues that need some discussion, like weight loss or going to church together. It's time to have a heart-to-heart talk with your spouse. Agree to make this the last time you will ever bring up the issue again unless your mate wants you to hold him or her accountable in this area. Express your feelings in the most sincere and strongest way you can without shaming or blaming your mate. (If you need help in how to phrase your feelings appropriately, see challenges 3 and 4.) Let him or her know how important this area is to you and how much it would mean to you if he or she could find a way to change this behavior. Offer your assistance and enthusiastic, not sarcastic, support if your mate is willing to try to change. And then let them know that your love will be steadfast even if they never change this behavior. That's all you can do. Now let it go. If your mate changes, great. It will be his or her gift of love to you. If they don't, you've done what you could, and now at least you can put it behind you.

For the very serious hurts and disappointments, we can't strongly enough recommend seeking some professional help. If you've already worked through your pain and disappointment, take pride in how far you've journeyed toward improving your relationship for the second half. Surviving marital strife with your relationship intact can only increase your potential for a loving, fulfilling marriage.

Change your responses. Now that you have forgiven your mate and once and for all let go, how will you respond to these same issues in the future? Most of the time, our reaction to our mate's perceived shortcomings is worse than whatever it was our mate did or did not do. The next time you sense irritation rising, try to turn the situation around by replacing your negative response with loving encouragement for your spouse. Choose to verbalize something positive to your mate each day.

"Wait a minute," a participant in our workshop interrupted. "This is way too hard. You don't know what you're asking us to do. You don't know all the history of hurts we have to overcome."

"I understand," another participant spoke up. "George and I have had our share of conflicts and angry words. For a while it looked as if our marriage was not going to make it, but both of us wanted it to survive. When our children left home, crisis hit. For a period of time, we went for counseling and worked through what we could. But at one point, we realized this was the best we could do. There were some dreams we would never realize. We simply had to let them go."

"Joyce is right," George said. "We decided to give our marriage a second chance. We realized we needed a new start, so we took all our old hurts and unfulfilled dreams and we threw them away. We forgave each other, and we agreed that each morning when we get out of bed, we will give each other a clean slate. Daily we choose not to carry over any hurts from the day before. We've been doing this now for a couple of years, and we're still together and making progress. Our marriage in the second half is different from the first half, and we're learning the rules and growing together."

Don't Limit Forgiveness

We realize that everybody doesn't place the same value on marriage. Not everyone has the patience or commitment of Jennifer. And George and Joyce also show wonderful tenacity. Sadly, our culture has embraced serial monogamy. Many couples tying the knot today will have several different marriage partners over their lifetime. But it doesn't have to be that way! Not if we are willing to generously oil our relationships with love and forgiveness.

All marriages need forgiveness and a big dose of reality. No spouse is perfect! Even when we are trying to please the other, we can mess up. For instance, one summer Claudia's birthday fell on a day when we were attending a conference in Fort Collins, Colorado. Dave, wanting to do something extra nice to celebrate, planned a nice weekend getaway to the nearby Rocky Mountains. But on the Saturday of that weekend—the actual day of Claudia's birthday—he totally forgot it was her day. At first she was irritated; then the longer he forgot, the angrier she became. When Dave tried to discover what was bugging her, her response was, "If you don't know, I certainly am not going to tell you!" Finally, having had her fill of misery, Claudia told Dave, "It's my birthday!" On that day she apologized first.

Do you have a squeaky marriage that needs the oil of forgiveness? We do. And it's not just Dave's wheel or Claudia's wheel that needs attention. We find that as we live out our love relationship daily, both of us need to forgive and ask the other for forgiveness. While we try to accept each other's little irritating habits, at times we react and need to ask for forgiveness.

Some situations are chronic—like the collection of clothes in our bathroom. "Dave," Claudia asked, "is there any reason you can't hang your clothes up at night before going to bed? I'm so tired of seeing your clothes draped over the chair every morning. Can't you be more considerate?"

"I'm being considerate," Dave answered. "You went to bed early, and I didn't want to wake you by opening the closet door or turning on the light. Anyway, what's the big deal? You leave your clothes there, too."

"Not all of the time—not as much as you do!" Claudia snapped back.

We never had this problem in our old house—our bathroom was too small. But there were plenty of other things to be irritated about. You probably have your own list. The little daily things are like little gnats swarming around us. How can we swat the gnats without swatting each other?

Acceptance and forgiveness are vital, but in long-term marriages, we also need to add kindness and compassion. Colossians 3:12–14 says,

> Therefore, as God's chosen people, holy and dearly loved, clothe yourselves with compassion, kindness, humility, gentleness and patience. Bear with each other and forgive whatever grievances you may have against one another. Forgive as the Lord forgave you. And over all these virtues put on love, which binds them all together in perfect unity.

These are attributes of an enriched, growing long-term marriage. All are needed if the second half of marriage is going to be the better half.

WHERE ARE YOU?

Where are you in your marriage? Maybe you are the Lone Ranger in trying to save your marriage. Maybe you even have grounds for divorce. Are you brave enough to forgive a spouse who doesn't want forgiveness? To accept your mate's little irritating habits that probably won't change? To give up unreachable dreams? To realize that every marriage relationship has disappointments? Are you brave enough to daily give the gift of love, compassion, and patience? Then we challenge you to renew your commitment to your marriage.

COMMITMENT TO GROWTH

Will you renew your commitment to your mate and make a commitment to grow together for the second half of your marriage? From our survey, we offer encouragement and hope to all of those who are in or are entering the second half of marriage. For those couples who choose to forgive and to grow together, we are happy to report that marital satisfaction goes up. For those couples, the best *is* yet to be!

Years ago as we sat on our screened porch, looking at our "we'll never do" list, we began to make another list. This is our "second half of marriage" list. It includes those things we choose to do to make the rest of our marriage the best. We share our list with you in hopes that you will adopt our list as your own.

Things We Will Do in the Second Half of Marriage

We will release and let go of our missed dreams and disappointments with each other, with our children, with our parents, and with ourselves.

We will accept each other as a package deal.

We will forgive and ask for forgiveness when needed.

We will renew our commitment to each other and to growing together in the second half of our marriage.

Wherever you are in your marriage, don't take your spouse for granted. Keep looking forward. Keep forgiving and asking for forgiveness. Keep on being patient with each other. Let compassion and kindness flow from your life to the love of your life. Keep dreaming and being willing to let go of missed dreams and release those little disappointments.

Recommit yourself to your spouse and to your marriage. You can handle disappointments and move on in your marriage. You can reconnect and rebuild your relationship. You can refocus on your mate and, in the process, become a loving and close companion.

MARRIAGE BUILDER

The Kindness-Compassion-Patience-Love-Forgiveness Test (Colossians 3:12–14)

1. Kindness: grace, generosity, friendliness, accommodation.
   How could you express kindness to your mate today, in your words and in your actions?

2. Compassion: tenderness, clemency, sympathy, commiseration.
   When was the last time you showed compassion for your spouse?

3. Patience: forbearance, submission, endurance, constancy, long-sufferingness.
   Has your patience become a little frayed? Is there a situation right now that would benefit from a big dose of patience?

4. Love: affection, charity, friendship, regard, devotion, benevolence, fervor.
   Love is not a nebulous emotion. Love is an attitude of caring more for the other person than for yourself. And love is expressed in little acts of kindness. List ways you have shown love in the past week.

5. Forgiveness: pardon, mercy, acquittal, absolution, reprieve, excuse.
   (We suggest you meditate alone on this part of the Marriage Builder exercise so it will remain a "marriage builder.")
   Are there things for which you need to ask your spouse for forgiveness?

   Is there something you need to forgive your spouse for?

6. Make a list:

   You may want to make a list of your mate's positive traits, just as you made a list of his or her shortcomings. Think about what is right about your marriage. What are the positive qualities of your spouse?

Challenge Two

※

*Create a Marriage That Is Partner-Focused
Rather Than Child-Focused*

–––––––––––––––––––– ∂∞ ––––––––––––––––––––

With two teenagers, I'm so overwhelmed that my marriage is on the back burner. I know I desperately need to refocus— but how? I'm so tired!

—wife married for eighteen years

I'm fearful that when our children leave home, we will go our separate ways, because our priorities and interests are so different.

—husband married for nineteen years

Build your marriage as the most important relationship, because that's what you have when the kids leave home.

—husband married for thirty-nine years

It's important to build a good relationship with your spouse so that when the children leave, you have the underlying joy of focusing on each other and not on your adult children.

—wife married for thirty-three years

The sense of being part of a couple is what consolidates modern marriage. It is the strongest rampart against the relentless threat of our divorce culture.

—Judith Wallerstein[1]

Having spent the last quarter of a century relating in thirty-second sound bites as we handed off car keys, ate quick bites of pizza, and scrambled to keep up with our children's hectic schedules, spending an entire evening together without interruption seemed like a challenge rather than a treat. What would we talk about? Did we have anything in common besides our kids and our work? How would we redefine our roles now that our kids were gone?

We faced a new era in our relationship. We had looked forward to being just two again, but now that we were, we needed to redefine our relationship. During the parenting years, our relationship was focused around the demands of parenting and career rather than around our marriage. Now that our children were grown, we no longer had their activities or crises as a focus. We had time to carry on a conversation, take a walk, whatever.

We felt uneasy with all of this time together. We were conditioned to feel guilty if we weren't doing two things at once. And we quickly realized that our old style of relating was not going to be sufficient. Books like our *60 One-Minute Marriage Builders* were great, but now we could relate in larger blocks of time. If we were to survive all this additional togetherness, we were going to have to deepen our friendship and build a relationship that was centered around each other. Of course, for us workaholics, the temptation was great to simply refocus our marriage from children to activities and to our work in family enrichment and get right back on the marital roller coaster.

THE MARITAL ROLLER COASTER

As we've said before, transitional times can be dangerous for a marriage. There are crisis points that, unless carefully managed, will result in the breakup of a marriage. Most couples are reasonably satisfied at the beginning of their marriage (we got along great for the four years before we had children). As children arrive, marital happiness tends to decline. The arrival of our first baby complicated our relationship. Passion, romance, and excitement were temporarily replaced by pain, exhaustion, and little togetherness.

Some couples at this stage—where stress is high and marital satisfaction low—decide to call it quits. However, within three or four years, they often remarry and take on the greater stress of a blended family.

Another time of marital dissatisfaction is when children enter the teen years. Often parents become so overwhelmed by the turbulence of the adolescent years that they put their marriage on the back burner. Then when the kids leave home, one mate bails out as well.

Our friend Kelly told us, "I used to wonder why so many people divorced after thirty years of marriage. How could anyone throw away such a long-term marriage? Then our last child left home, and we learned this isn't an easy time in life. For the first time, we had time to finish a conversation and even finish an argument. My husband, Charlie, was terrified!"

DIFFERENT GROWTH RATES

One cause of midlife breakups is mates growing at different rates. Have you heard it said, "They simply outgrew each other" or "They just don't have anything in common"?

In public Frank and Sue were the happy couple, but in private both were dissatisfied with their midlife marriage. Sue focused her life on the children and community activities, while Frank, a nuclear scientist, lived in his own world of atoms and particles. Their intellectual interests were worlds apart. Financially they were comfortable. They loved their children, but the prospect of living together without the kids around made them apprehensive. Their limited time together was usually devoted to the details of the day. Real communication was scarce. Yet everyone was surprised when, as their last child headed for college, Frank and Sue headed for the divorce court.

A marriage may be functional, but a relationship without emotional intimacy is certainly not exciting and is all too often terminal. Yet the good news is that for couples who survive the empty nest and choose to refocus their marriage on their partner, marital satisfaction again rises. But be prepared for changes!

SWITCHING ROLES

As you begin the second half of marriage, roles may switch. Rules may change. At this time of life, many wives become more focused and assertive and are eager to try their professional wings—especially if they dedicated the first half of life to nurturing and parenting their children. Some women pursue educational studies. About this time, most husbands decide to slow down and enjoy life a little bit more. For men at fifty, work is not so important.

Gail Sheehy, in her book *New Passages*, describes it this way:

> A massive shift takes place across gender lines as we grow older. What is observable empirically is that women begin to be more focused, more interested in tasks and accomplishments than in nurturing, whereas men start to show greater interest in nurturing and being nurtured. . . . Women become more independent and assertive, men more expressive and emotionally responsive. These changes in middle and later life are developmental, not circumstantial, and they occur in predictable sequences across widely disparate cultures.[2]

Changes, when handled wisely, can enhance a second-half marriage. Sheehy says that the day we turn forty-five should be considered the infancy of another life. We should embrace a second adulthood—one in which new passages lead to new creativity, deeper meaning, and renewed playfulness. We suggest embracing a new marriage as well (but with the same partner!). But change does not come without some confusion.

On one occasion, our phone rang and a Boston attorney facing the second half of his marriage was on the line: "My wife says she doesn't love me anymore. What did I do that was so wrong? I've never had affairs. We've both been good parents and supportive of our children, but they are growing up. One is in college and the other in high school. And now my wife says she's bored and doesn't love me anymore. She wants to move to New York and go to graduate school. I'm dumbfounded! By profession, I'm an attorney, I fix things. Why didn't my wife just tell me what she wanted me to do? If she wanted conversation, all she had to do was to say so. If she wanted to go to fancy restaurants, she only had to ask. There's a gap here I wasn't aware of. If she will just tell me what I need to do to fix it, I'll do it, but I don't have a clue what to do!"

THE MIDLIFE SEARCH FOR INTIMACY AND COMPANIONSHIP

How can we fix long-term marriages that are troubled? How can we refocus? What can we do in midlife to promote growth and intimacy? Our mentor Dr. David Mace, who is a behavioral scientist, writes,

> We need to understand clearly that a relationship of intimacy only becomes possible between two people when they are able to take down their defenses, open up their inner selves, and make themselves vulnerable to each other. This is actually what intimacy really means, as the term "shared privacy" suggests.[3]

Yet many couples facing the second half of marriage have little shared privacy. Their private lives have been consumed with their children and careers. Now they enter a new stage of life with new responsibilities and priorities. How can they take Dr. Mace's advice and open themselves up to each other in a more intimate way?

BECOMING CLOSE COMPANIONS

This kind of intimacy is possible in what Dr. Mace calls a "companionship marriage," wherein marriage is a partnership. Dr. Mace defines companionship marriage in the following way:

> Companionship marriage is a socially registered commitment between a man and a woman, in which they seek to know themselves and each other as far as they are capable of being known, and, through mutual affection and affirmation, help each other to grow and change in order to become the loving and creative persons they are capable of becoming.[4]

One wife wrote on her survey, "My husband is my best friend, my companion. We can talk about everything, and we really enjoy each other's company. Somehow we have avoided power plays in our relationship and make most decisions together." In a companionship marriage, each trusts the other so the full blossoming of love and tenderness can be achieved. This sounds ideal, but is it achievable for couples in the second half? Our answer is an emphatic "Yes!" But it takes work. It doesn't happen automatically. And it has more to do with the quality of the relationship than the style of the marriage.

Some couples are more comfortable with defined roles and functions for husband and wife. This traditional style of marriage, in which both partners have their areas of responsibilities, may work well when the children are growing up, careers are taking off, and the most efficient way is to "divide and conquer." However, while it may be congenial, this style offers less emotional intimacy.

Other couples work toward a complete sharing of responsibility, decision making, and even parenting. This style of marriage is more egalitarian or democratic. In the second half of marriage, as roles change and partners seek a closer, more intimate relationship, a couple may move closer to this style. They may experience a deeper level of commonality and friendship, but marriage will be more complicated, and there will inevitably be much more open conflict to resolve.

Whatever style of marriage you choose—traditional or egalitarian—for the second half of marriage you need to become more partner focused. And as Dr. Mace challenges us, you need to become close companions.

BECOMING MORE PARTNER FOCUSED

Recently we took a break from writing and went to our favorite greenway for a walk. As we've mentioned, we do some of our best thinking when we are walking, so on this day we decided to brainstorm. "When we think of a partner-focused marriage—or as Dr. Mace defined it, a companionship marriage," Claudia asked, "what are some distinguishing characteristics?"

"First," Dave started, "I would say that a companionship marriage is one in which both spouses are encouraged to maximize their strengths for the benefit of the couple."

"'For the benefit of the couple,'" interrupted Claudia. "That's key! So many marriages are centered around what is best for the individual, not the couple. So it's more of an attitude of putting the marriage first. Using your diversity to create couple unity."

"How would this play out in a second-half marriage?" Dave asked.

"Well," Claudia answered, "let's think of couples we know who are in the second half of marriage and whose marriage style we would consider 'companionship.'"

About that time, Letta and Gerald Yardman walked by. We winked at each other, knowing we had answered our own question. The Yardmans—older than us by several years—were definitely in the second half. Their youngest child, their late-life surprise, was still in high school. Still, they found the time every day for their two-mile walk.

Both Letta and Gerald had participated in our survey. Both considered companionship and friendship to be a high priority in their thirty-eight-year marriage. They were deeply committed to each other, but things much deeper than that commitment kept their marriage on a growing course. They definitely weren't just tolerating each other. They enjoyed being together!

Their children, parents, friends, jobs, and hobbies were important, but none were as important as their marriage. While they were compatible, they certainly didn't agree on everything. "Conflict is actually good for our marriage," Letta told us. "Sometimes it's a challenge to find a solution we can both live with, but we are determined never to manipulate or pull a power play. Our marriage is far too precious to jeopardize it just to try to get our own way."

THE OTHER SIDE

"Let's look at the other side," Dave said to Claudia after the Yardmans had gone. "How would you describe a marriage that is not as partner focused or companionship based?"

"Hmm." Claudia was silent for a few moments and then said, "When both spouses want their own way, they don't have a companionship or partner-focused marriage. Sometimes one spouse is active, the other spouse passive. Or there's little passion, intimacy, or sense of we-ness."

"Or the marriage," Dave added, "is being held together by their commitment to never give up no matter how bad it gets. Those who responded to our survey and said that the best thing about their marriage was their children or anything other than their spouse would be in this category."

"It would also include those who said that the best thing about their marriage was their commitment, but everything else indicated a low level of marital satisfaction."

Other research confirms our findings. Scott Stanley, Ph.D., a clinical psychologist at the University of Denver who specializes in research on marriage, said,

> Commitment can keep a couple together. But commitment based on constraint alone makes for a pretty miserable marriage.... Marriages don't have to slide into a state of 'committed misery.' But to avoid it, spouses have to nurture dedication for a lifetime.[5]

MUTUAL ADJUSTMENT IS VITAL

One way we nurture our marriage is by continually adjusting to each other and striving to be partner focused. The survival of a long-term marriage depends on the complex process of mutual adjustment of the two people to each other. And whatever your marriage style, you need to adjust and refocus on each other and shore up your friendship.

In our survey, each age group said that the best aspect of their marriage was companionship, but as age increased, so did the importance of companionship. For those under age fifty, 31 percent rated companionship as the best aspect, but for those fifty and over, the percentage jumped to 43 percent.

At this stage, marriage must be held together from within—from the inner core of the relationship. There are few pressures outside a marriage that are strong enough to influence a couple to stay in a marriage that isn't functioning and in which the couple are miserable. The answer is to build healthy, enriched marriages that can hold together from within.

A strength of the companionship marriage is having a strong sense of being part of a couple. It is critical in the second half of marriage to develop a sense of we-ness. Judith Wallerstein, in her book *The Good Marriage*, writes, "We-ness gives marriage its staying power in the face of life's inevitable frustrations and temptations to run away or stray."[6]

REDEFINING OUR ROLES

As we began the second half of our marriage, we looked for ways to develop we-ness. Everything seemed to be changing, so we took advantage of this transitional time to regroup and reconnect. While Dave had participated around the home as a parent and partner, running the household had mainly been Claudia's responsibility. During the adolescent years, we used a cleaning service on a regular basis. Now with just the two of us and with bills for college tuition, we decided to discontinue our cleaning service. Neither of us is energized by housework. While over the years Claudia had done more than her share, we now had the opportunity to make an adjustment. Claudia was elated. Dave was apprehensive. We both saw it as an opportunity to promote we-ness and equality.

First we listed all the various jobs and chores. Then we discussed the list from the standpoint of who can do the job better. Claudia immediately conceded that Dave was the best bathroom cleaner in ten states! Yet we discovered that if we attacked our house together, we got through the dirty jobs, and neither felt we had to do it all alone. Claudia still had the edge as chief chef, but we named Dave as chief bottle washer! And in our desire to work together, Dave agreed to learn some culinary skills.

On occasion, we even grocery shop together. (Claudia knows that if Dave goes alone to the grocery store, he may forget the milk and bread but will come home with enough snacks to feed our entire neighborhood. Dave, on the other hand, says that Claudia's solo grocery store visits result in every new low-fat, no-salt, no-taste product on the market.) Going together helps us develop we-ness, especially if we go to our favorite market, which plays classical music and serves gourmet coffee!

Our friends Freda and Pete make the bed together each morning. "This is our time," Freda told us, "when we talk and connect with each other. Even if I'm in the kitchen, Pete will call me to come make up the bed together! It's just a little thing, but it helps us focus on each other."

What little things can you do to develop we-ness and focus on your spouse? In the second half of marriage, we can share rather than divide. Maybe the one who handles all the finances can share the load with the other. Or if you're the cook, let your mate prepare one meal a week, or try cooking as a duo.

Or you could take a more drastic approach. Switch roles for a week and discover what areas you would like to redistribute and share together. Our friend Bob does the grocery shopping. His wife, Barbara, is the superorganized detail person. She is a thorough, competent grocery shopper, but a trip to the market for Barbara could consume hours! She gets so involved in the details—which brand is the most nutritious for the lowest price—that she forgets the time. So Barbara sees Bob's action as focusing on the "we" in their marriage.

ONE CAUTION!

In a companionship marriage, couples have greater expectations for their marriage relationship. Their quest for intimacy leads to a degree of closeness that at the same time can generate conflict. A companionship marriage is more complicated and much more work, but it is worth the effort! As we begin the second half of marriage, life changes, like it or not. The dynamics of the relationship in the second half of marriage cannot remain the same, but these changes can be opportunities for growth.

FLY JETS!

One of Dr. Mace's favorite illustrations of why a companionship marriage is desirable has to do with aeronautics. He reminds us what happened when we made the switch from piston-engine planes to jet-engine planes. The new planes were superior in every way. They could fly higher and faster and were much more comfortable. However, when the transition took place, all the pilots had to be retrained. Jet-engine planes were far more complicated, and the retraining of the pilots was critical. If they had simply put pilots in the jet planes and told them to just do their best, jet planes would have been crashing all over the place!

This is what is happening to marriages as they reach the second half. Traditional marriages are less complicated but don't have a lot of closeness. They could be compared to the piston-engine plane. Now, in the second half of their marriage, most couples want a deeper, more personal marriage relationship. They want to move up to the jet engine, but like the pilots, they need to be retrained. They need to learn new relational skills to succeed in communicating on a deeper level and using conflict constructively.

But too often, when couples enter the uncharted years of the second half of marriage, they try to have jet-engine marriages without having any knowledge about how to build a deeper and more personal relationship. No wonder marriages are crashing all around us! Retraining is necessary, but first we need to realize that a change of relationship dynamics within marriage is occurring as we begin the second half. Next we must learn the necessary skills to succeed in the new, jet kind of relationship.[7] It's time to upgrade our relationship, fly jets, and focus on each other. We can do this by developing a second-half coping system.

SECOND-HALF COPING SYSTEM

With our Christian faith and our commitment to each other as our foundation, we have adopted a coping system that has allowed us to grow in intimacy, to work through conflict and anger, and to build a true companionship marriage. Our coping system, which we learned from our mentors, Drs. David and Vera Mace, contains three essentials for a growing marriage:

1. A commitment to growth
2. An effectively functioning communication system
3. The ability to make creative use of conflict[8]

Daily we reaffirm our commitment to continued growth in our marriage. This is the first essential part of our coping system. Our marriage is fluid and requires a daily investment of time and energy. Without that investment, you can have a long-term marriage, but it will probably be dull and boring! The cornerstone of a successful second-half marriage is giving each other the freedom to grow, knowing that the marriage *will* survive no matter what and that your commitment to each other is for a lifetime. Challenge 1 emphasized the commitment to having a growing, living marriage.

The second essential part of our coping system is having a communication system that works. Keeping our communication open and sharing our feelings freely with each other—though not easy to do— is a high priority. For years, when our children were underfoot, communication often was in memos or thirty-second messages on answering machines. It can be scary when suddenly you have uninterrupted time to complete a conversation or talk about a difficult subject! Effective communication is essential if you want to enjoy this new time in life. In challenge 3 we'll look at how you can hone your communication skills.

The third essential part of our coping system is our commitment to work through our disagreements and each angry situation that arises. From the Maces we learned that both love *and* anger are positive forces in building a healthy marriage. They give balance and keep us from becoming enmeshed. Every marriage has conflict. Yet too often, in the middle of conflict, anger explodes and destroys, rather than builds, the marriage relationship. So we must learn to positively process anger and release its energy to grow our relationship. In challenge 4 we'll talk more about how to process anger in the second half of marriage.

Transition times in marriage provide us with opportunities to test our coping system! Adjustments are often needed, especially at the beginning of the second half of marriage.

MEET ESTHER AND RALPH

At a neighborhood party, we met Esther and Ralph, who were a living example of a couple who had successfully met the challenge to refocus on each other. Their coping system was functioning, and they had a spark in their relationship that had not always been there. Here is their story:

"When our kids left home, we didn't know each other," Ralph commented.

"It was frightening," Esther added. "We were strangers. For years the children had been our focus. We were good parents. We set goals for our children but never considered setting goals for our marriage. Our lives revolved around our kids and their activities. We had few conflicts; we got along. We loved each other, but when the kids left home, there was a vacuum. We realized we didn't know each other. It was a crisis time in our marriage."

"Plus, the rules changed," Ralph continued. "Esther changed. In the past, Esther was passive; she went along with what I wanted. But when the kids left home, she began to speak up—to be more assertive. I didn't know what was happening!"

"For the first time," Esther went on, "I could concentrate on my career, which really started to take off. This gave me more confidence to speak up. For years my identity was my role as a mother. Now I had a whole new world to discover."

"This was confusing for me," added Ralph. "I was experiencing problems with my heart and wanted to slow down in my job and spend more time at home, but Esther was just getting the wind in her professional sails! I tried to talk to her, but we really didn't know how to communicate."

"It was scary," Esther said slowly, "very scary!"

"But you made it," Dave commented. "We've been observing you all evening, and you like each other. You enjoy being together and have a close relationship. What happened?"

Ralph responded, "We took time to redefine our marriage. We realized our old roles no longer applied. There were old hurts to overcome; we had to forgive each other. We gave up some old dreams, but at the same time, we made a commitment to grow closer to each other."

"And," Esther added, "we worked hard to rebuild our relationship and develop new communication skills. We invested time in each other and learned how to enjoy one another's company again. Basically, when the kids left, there was no relationship. So we looked for things to do together. Since we lived near several lakes, we took up boating, which was relaxing and easy on Ralph's heart."

"Our mutual activities," Ralph added, "helped us build a friendship bridge to the second half of our marriage. Now we realize we should have taken time all along the way to build our marriage. When the kids came along and were growing up, we didn't have the money for dinner out, but looking back, we could have done other things that didn't require money."

THE CHALLENGE TO REFOCUS

Do you identify with Esther and Ralph's story? Be encouraged; wherever you are in your relationship, you can start today to refocus on your spouse. You can reevaluate your roles. You can build a companionship marriage. While growth may cause some disruption in the marital relationship, as you grow and seek to become more partner focused, your marriage can be strengthened. Marriage in the second half can be much more fulfilling as you work for the benefit of the couple and as you become better friends and close companions.

In the next two chapters, we'll look at love and anger in a second-half marriage and at how to communicate in a way that will facilitate becoming both close companions and best friends. You are already in the process of making the rest of your marriage the best!

———————— ❧ ————————

MARRIAGE BUILDER

Question for Reflection: Creating a More Partner-Focused Marriage

Following are some reflective questions to think about and mull over. Why not invite your mate to go with you to your favorite coffee shop, and over two cups of coffee or cappuccino, you can talk about the following things. Go on and take the challenge. Your marriage is worth it!

1. On a scale of one to ten (ten being the most), how much we-ness do you have in your marriage relationship?

2. How would you describe your marriage style?

3. What opportunities have you taken to grow your marriage?
   —In the first half of your marriage?

   —In the last twelve months?

4. Have you redefined your roles for the second half?

5. What are some things you can do to develop a more partner-focused marriage?

6. What opportunities for growth are you facing in your marriage at the present time?

7. Would you be willing to read one book dealing with an area of your marriage in which you would like to grow?

Challenge Three

❧

Maintain an Effective Communication
System That Allows You to Express Your Deepest
Feelings, Joys, and Concerns

—————————— ❧ ——————————

*My greatest fear is that when the kids are gone, we won't
communicate or have anything in common. I'm afraid of being
left alone with someone who never speaks, pays attention,
or ever touches me.*

—wife married for eighteen years

*Learn how to talk about those things that really matter to you.
Communication and intimacy can grow in a love relationship.*

—wife married for forty-seven years

*The greatest stress in my marriage is lack of communication—
just being able to converse at the end of the day. I always feel as if
I'm competing with the computer, the newspaper, or CNN news.*

—wife married for seven years, second marriage

*The greatest frustration for me in my marriage is simply
not being understood.*

—wife married for fifteen years

*I enjoy being with her, looking at her, walking with her,
and talking to her.*

—husband married for nineteen years

Communication is not a matter of being right but of starting a flow of energy between two people that can result in mutual understanding.

—John A. Sanford[1]

"System overload" described life at the Arps'. Here's the situation: it was 1:00 a.m.; we were leaving early the next morning to speak at a Sam's Warehouse national convention; we still needed to pack. While this scenario was stressful enough to challenge our empty nest communication skills, there is more to this story.

Rewind one week: Our family two-story home—complete with memories, a list of maintenance repairs, and a half-acre yard to mow and maintain—was more house than just the two of us needed and more house than we could manage. Quite by accident, on a Sunday afternoon drive we found a half-constructed single-dwelling condo—the house of our dreams. Dave loved the thought of no yard work. Claudia loved the open plan and spacious master suite on the first floor. So being the spontaneous people that we are, a couple of days later we signed on the dotted line.

Now back to where we started. The real estate people were coming the next day (while we were gone) to evaluate the old home place. While family memories topped our "value list," the real estate company valued appearance—order and cleanliness were at the top of their list. We had spent the day cleaning and organizing. Feeling quite successful, we were ready to crawl in bed when Claudia happened to peek into our laundry room. In a pile on the floor lay some dirty clothes she had forgotten to wash. Being the creative one, she thought, *No problem, I'll put them in our storage shed*. Which she did.

After returning from our speaking engagement, we threw ourselves totally into picking out tile, carpet, paint, and wallpaper for our condo, and planning our upcoming move. We forgot about our dirty clothes in the storage shed until several weeks later, when Dave asked, "Claudia, have you seen my favorite khaki shorts?"

Yelp! They were in the storage shed, mildewing with our other clothes!

Why are we telling you about our dirty laundry? It's a great picture of what sometimes happens to marital communication in the second half of marriage. It's easy to get so involved with life challenges that we let our communication slide. Issues we need to discuss pile up like our dirty clothes, and then when we're most stressed out (like late at night), we trip over them. Too tired to deal with them, we stuff them in our marriage storage shed, where they sour and mildew. It's no mystery why so many couples seem to grow apart and wonder what to do with all those quiet evenings!

When we settle for shallow conversations and don't deal with real issues, the prognosis of our long-term marriage is not encouraging. Ray and Anne Ortlund, in their book *The Best Half of Life*, write,

> All of us married people have to realize that time is a corrosive influence. We don't naturally drift closer together; we drift further apart. We have to fight our way back to each other, day after day, year after year, as long as we live. Across the board, in marriages that survive, the evidence seems to be that in every succeeding decade of the average marriage, the partners are less satisfied with each other and with their marriage! They no longer talk as much, interact as much. Strangers under the same roof, they live in increasing loneliness. Yet both have needs for love as great as ever—maybe greater.[2]

One new empty nest wife put it this way: "How can just the two of us fill a table for five? There is such a void in our lives. We eat breakfast in silence and stare at each other and the three empty places. Since the kids are gone, we don't really have anything to talk about. How can we reconnect and get reacquainted?"

A husband married for thirty-four years said, "My greatest fear is that we will live out our lives in the same house but living in separate spaces."

And a wife married for nine years wrote, "I fear that our marriage will continue as it is or get worse. We seldom have a real conversation."

Maybe we should offer a refresher course for tired midlife marriages. It could be done as part of your child's college application process. Maybe the parents of the college applicant should have to write an essay on their marriage potential and communication skills.

We can all identify with some of the universal conversation blockers: the time crunch, work overload, a stressful lifestyle, parenting and extended family responsibilities, sports and hobbies, television, sports on television . . . Our list could go on and on. But what about the communication patterns that we have used over the years that seemed to work while the children were around? Now as the children begin leaving the nest, our old ways of communicating don't seem to be working. There is more silence, less to say to each other. The children—those wonderful buffers—no longer offer comic relief. You may ask yourself, *We made it this far. Why is it now so difficult to have a really personal conversation—and without becoming negative?*

WASHED-OUT COMMUNICATION

In the closeness of a marriage relationship, we all exchange negative communication from time to time. But Dr. John Gottman, professor of psychology at the University of Washington in Seattle, in his book *Why Marriages Succeed or Fail*, writes, "For a marriage to last there must be at least five positive interactions for every negative one between partners."[3]

Sometimes we don't make that ratio. We go too far in expressing our negative feelings and experience what Dr. Gottman refers to as "system overload" or "feeling flooded." When this happens, you feel overwhelmed by your spouse's negativity. You may feel defensive, hostile, or just want to withdraw and go into your shell.

Dr. Gottman suggests that we each have a sort of built-in meter that measures how much negativity accumulates during our conversations.

How much you can handle before "flooding" depends on your own personality and is also affected by how much stress you're already under. He has observed that men tend to become flooded far more easily than women, and this may explain the classic male reaction of stonewalling. However, women can also feel flooded.

How does it feel when you are flooded? You may feel misunderstood, unfairly attacked, wronged, or righteously indignant. Dr. Gottman points out that there are also physical symptoms. It may be hard to breathe. You may tend to hold your breath. Have you ever done that when you are in the middle of an argument? Muscles may tense up and the heart may beat faster. What you desperately want is relief.[4]

PERSONALLY THREATENED

When you begin to talk about personal things, it's easy to feel threatened. Americans seem to admire the impersonal side of life: accomplishments, achievements, financial success, houses, cars, boats, and athletics. But talking about our personal lives is disdained. Impersonal things take less effort, while the personal side of life, which includes close relationships, is too time intensive. Americans are too busy for life! Having lived for a number of years in Europe, we've seen a contrast between Europeans and Americans. Everything takes longer in Europe. If you go to a restaurant, you go for the whole evening. In American restaurants, it's in and out, like an assembly line. We want quick fixes—and quick fixes offer little opportunity for intimate conversations or romance.

Our culture is missing romance—especially in the second half of marriage. In Vienna, we saw so many older couples out walking together, holding hands and talking. Go to a mall or park here—where are the couples? Where are the couples who like each other and are having intimate conversations? If you would like to be one of those couples in the second half of your marriage, we have two suggestions:

1. Start by evaluating your present communication pattern.

2. Learn how to talk on a more personal level by sharing your feelings with one another.

WHAT'S YOUR COMMUNICATION PATTERN?

When the children leave home (even if they return), things change. Communication patterns that worked during the first half of marriage are often found inadequate and lacking for the second half. But before we can explore new ways of personally connecting, let's look at why the old ways aren't working anymore. Let's consider several communication patterns that reflect how typical couples deal with the deeper issues—including those areas that cause tension in the relationship. (In the next chapter, we will deal with how to handle conflict and process anger. At this point, we only want to identify our patterns of communication.)

The Avoider-Confronter Couple

Meet Ruth and Sam. From the beginning of their marriage, there were unresolved issues. When they tried to talk about serious issues like education and career plans or in-laws, or less important issues like who is going to wash the dishes or take out the garbage, their communication patterns were different. Ruth was the confrontive one, while Sam was the avoider.

Ruth and Sam were married while they were in college. Sam's overbearing mother didn't help their communication. Ruth thought Sam should stand up to her and tell her to mind her own business. Sam just wanted Ruth to stop complaining and ignore his mother.

Sam was uncomfortable with emotional talk. He'd had that all his life from his mother. Ruth's family let it all hang out, so she was extremely verbal. She would express how she felt, and if Sam didn't respond, she would say it in a different way. Soon Sam just turned her off and retreated into his own world.

Children came along and Ruth threw her energies into parenting. In other mothers, she found friends who liked intense conversations and would listen and respond to her. Sam sure didn't.

Where was Sam emotionally during this time? Sam's lack of ability to tolerate Ruth's flood of negative feelings and emotional talk kept him in his shell and drove him to those who would listen to him with no emotional demands. Unfortunately, this led over the years to a string of affairs.

Enter their own children's adolescent years, and things heated up even more. Ruth wanted Sam to go with her for counseling. She felt things would eventually work out for them, but they needed help. Sam refused to admit there was a problem. But one day Sam packed his bags and left. Eighteen years of marriage down the drain.

Sam's pattern of avoiding and Ruth's pattern of confronting represent a very common marital pattern and one that our culture reinforces, starting in childhood. According to Dr. Gottman,

> From early childhood, boys learn to suppress their emotions, while girls learn to express and manage the complete range of feelings. . . . A man is more likely to equate being emotional with weakness and vulnerability, because he has been raised to do rather than to voice what he feels. Meanwhile, women have spent their early years learning how to verbalize all kinds of emotions.[5]

Not only are there psychological differences, but, Dr. Gottman believes, marital communication patterns have a physiological basis as well. He notes,

> In order to fully understand why husbands and wives so often miss each other's needs, we have to recognize that the sexes may be physically programmed to react differently to emotional conflict—beginning in childhood.[6]

Dr. Gottman's research reveals that during conflict or emotional stress, a man's blood pressure and heart rate rises much higher and stays elevated longer than his wife's. Also, the male's autonomic nervous system, which controls much of the body's stress response, may be more sensitive. He points out that since men are more biologically reactive to stress, they are (like Sam) more likely to try to protect themselves by withdrawing and being distant.[7]

Think back on the first half of your marriage. Do you identify with Ruth? Do you identify with Sam? Were you the avoider, like Sam, or the confronter, like Ruth? What's your mate's style?

The Conflict-Avoiding Couple

When we met Anna and Martin, we often wondered how they ever got together. They were total opposites. Martin was outgoing and very charismatic, while Anna was very quiet and reserved. Martin was the dynamic leader of a parachurch organization and traveled extensively, while Anna had her own cottage industry business. Their three daughters were delightful and about all that Martin and Anna had in common.

When we were together with Anna and Martin, their relationship seemed to be a pleasant but distant one. While they seemed quite remote from each other, we never observed much tension or conflict. They lived under one roof but in separate worlds. We wondered how this marriage ever happened.

Unfortunately, when their daughters left home, they began to wonder, too. The distance between them became greater, until one day Martin left.

After Martin quit his marriage, we learned of his affair with someone in his office. Not only was Martin's marriage wrecked but so was his promising future with his missions organization. How much better to work at developing more intimacy with your mate. The second half of marriage is the perfect time to do that!

Some conflict-avoiding couples are distant from each other in their personal relationship but are close in other areas. They may actually work together well, but careers and other activities are the center of their lives and consume most of their time. Little is left over for their personal relationship. While their marriage is low on intimacy, they have a deep commitment to the permanence of their marriage and would never consider divorce. Dr. Gottman writes,

> One of the greatest strengths of a conflict-avoiding marriage is the ability to endure periodic turbulence based on the certainty that your relationship is built on a rock-solid foundation of common beliefs and values.[8]

In our survey, we observed that many couples who fit into this pattern of communication were from very conservative churches. They rated their common beliefs and their commitment to God and to their long-term marriage as the most important aspects of their marriage, while their communication, conflict resolution, and emotional closeness ratings were at very low levels of satisfaction.

Dr. Gottman's advice to conflict-avoiding couples is,

> While you may cherish the peaceful nature of your relationship above all else, you could be stifling too much negative emotion and not getting your needs met as individuals. When this happens, you risk becoming hostile and detached from one another. Some psychologists even theorize that conflict-avoiding couples suffer more physical ailments than others as a result of living with unresolved problems. If you turn all negative feelings inward, you're left with chronic, low-lying stress that eats away at your health and the stability of your marriage.[9]

Another danger of a marriage with little intimacy or closeness, as we saw with Martin, is the susceptibility to adulterous affairs. It feels good to have someone listen and show personal interest. If your marriage fits the conflict-avoiding pattern, we plead with you to take the steps to improve your ability to handle the negative feelings that inevitably crop up in any marriage relationship. You can improve the likelihood that your marital bond will remain stable. Later in this chapter, we talk about getting in touch with and learning to express your feelings. If you are the type of person who has not focused much on your emotions, it will take some practice before you can articulate what you feel to your mate, but keep on till you are able to do so. The life of your marriage may depend on it!

The Conflict-Confronting Couple

You always knew when Peg and Ron were around; you could hear them arguing! They communicated continually, but it was with disagreements and conflict—not unlike a display of fireworks. As the administrator for a large international organization, Ron was a competent contributor to the company. But on the home front, it was war! We wondered how they kept their marriage together. Actually, they were fun people to be around and always had lots of friends. But one on one, they just couldn't agree on anything. Though it was rocky, they made it through the first half of their marriage—but after their two sons left for college, Peg moved out. They still stay in touch. Ron says he thinks they will eventually get back together.

The problem with the confronting pattern is that venting your emotions causes them to escalate. Confrontations lead to counterconfrontations, and soon you may find yourself in a shouting match and saying things you later regret. Remember the old refrain "Sticks and stones may break my bones, but words will never harm me"? It just isn't true! Words do harm, and the confronting pattern of communication has many casualties.

The dilemma is this: avoiding issues causes space in the relationship; confronting them often results in discord and conflict. How can couples in the second half of marriage retool their communication patterns so they can resolve real issues and have intimate conversations for two? There is a fourth communication pattern. It is more difficult to cultivate; it takes hard work. But it is worth it. You can become an interpersonally competent couple!

THE INTERPERSONALLY COMPETENT COUPLE

Whatever your communication patterns have been in the past, for the second half of marriage you need to develop a more personal one—one that builds on your desire for companionship and we-ness, one that transcends your own tendency, cultural conditioning, or personality.

Sometimes we assume that communication difficulties are caused by our temperament or personality differences. Books like John Gray's *Men Are From Mars; Women Are From Venus* can be very informative and helpful in understanding basic differences in men and women, but at the heart of intimacy is the ability to develop interpersonal competency.

One couple from our survey are using their differences to develop interpersonal competence. The wife told us, "While we are quite different, we have a lot in common and both value our marriage above our individual interests and our careers. Although we are both strong-willed and opinionated, we have influenced each other to be more balanced in some areas. For example, I'm now more logical in decision making, because he's methodical and logical. I think he's become more openly compassionate, notices certain details, and is more appreciative of the artistic side of life because of my influence."

No stage of marriage has greater potential for developing interpersonal competence than the second half of marriage. And you have already taken the first step in becoming an interpersonally competent person if you have committed yourself to having a growing companionship marriage. This commitment should provide security in knowing that you desire your marriage to grow and are willing to open up to your spouse in a more intimate way.

How can you do this? By developing what family sociologist Nelson Foote calls "interpersonal competence."[10] If we want intimacy in our marriages, then we need to develop interpersonal intimacy—a personal closeness and the feeling of security and support that comes from closeness. But this is difficult to do in our culture. The tendency is to guard our inner thoughts, feelings, and wishes and try to hide our weaknesses. We wear masks in order to hide our real selves. "What we need, and need desperately," Foote says, "is a protected inner world in which we can take off our masks, relax, and learn to develop our hidden potential as loving, caring persons."[11]

The first step toward becoming an interpersonally competent couple is learning how to communicate your inner thoughts, feelings, and wishes in the context of this supportive relationship, in which you will be loved and accepted. These skills will enable you to resist confronting or avoiding each other in a negative way, as perhaps you have done in the past. Here are seven simple guidelines for developing interpersonally competent communication. We hope they will help you as much as they have helped us.

Seven Tips for Talking on a More Personal Level

1. Learn to listen. An ad in a Kansas newspaper said, "I will listen to you talk without comment for thirty minutes for five dollars." Would you believe that ten to twenty people called every day from all over the United States just to have someone listen to them? This reaffirms how very important it is to have someone listen; in marriage, that someone needs to be your mate.

In James 1:19 we are told, "Everyone should be quick to listen, slow to speak and slow to become angry." In our actions, we too often rephrase this verse to, "Be slow to listen and very quick to speak and become angry." If we can slow our words and reactions, perhaps we could be better listeners. But don't just listen for the words—listen for the feelings as well.

2. Be aware of the nonverbal message. Several years ago Kodak did a study to determine what makes up the total message in interpersonal communication. Would you believe that over half of the message (55 percent) is nonverbal: the stares and glares and the smiles and the winks across the room? The tone of voice accounts for 38 percent of the message, and that only leaves 7 percent for the words! So the next personal conversation you have with your spouse, be aware of your total message. And make certain your nonverbal behavior, tone of voice, and words are saying the same thing. Nothing is worse than to hear the right words but sense underlying hostility, bitterness, and anger. Whatever your words, the nonverbal is the real message the other person hears.

3. Learn to communicate your feelings. Communication with your mate will never be really personal until you learn how to share your feelings with each other. In 1 Thessalonians 5:11 we read, "Therefore encourage one another and build each other up." Why are we hesitant in following this good advice?

In our culture, there is what the Maces call a "tenderness taboo." When we have tender thoughts about our spouse, often we think them but don't openly express them. How easy it is to express our negative feelings, but positive thoughts? We tend to hold the positive feelings inside—to think them but not say them. We need to express them.

But we also need to share our negative feelings. Our goal in expressing our negative feelings is to attack the problem, not the other person, but we must start with ourselves. We are responsible for what we say and how we say it, and it doesn't necessarily depend on how, or if, our mate responds. But we need a vocabulary of words to express feelings—both positive and negative. In our Marriage Alive seminar, we let the participants brainstorm "feelings words" and compile a list. They each develop their own feelings vocabulary. We've included both positive and negative words from their lists with the Marriage Builder exercise at the end of the chapter to help you share your feelings and communicate on a deeper level.

4. Use "I" statements; avoid "you" statements and "why" questions. "You" statements and "why" questions tend to be attacking, so you will want to avoid them. "I" statements are much safer. When you are making a statement, let it reflect back on you. You want to take responsibility for your own feelings.

There is a big difference between saying, "I feel so alone. Can we talk?" and saying, "You always ignore me. Why don't you ever talk with me?" The second example is a sure way to stop intimate conversations!

5. Learn to complete the communication cycle. When your spouse makes a statement, you can follow by saying, "What I hear you saying is . . ." At that point, your spouse can say, "Yes, that's what I meant" or "No, that's not what I meant at all!" Keep the communication cycle going until you both agree that what your spouse said is what you heard. This will greatly help your communication! Remember, your goal is to really understand what your spouse is saying and what he or she means by what is being said. Otherwise, your conversations will become what Paul Tournier describes as "dialogues of the deaf."

6. Agree not to attack the other person or to defend yourself. We have a simple contract that in talking with each other, we will not attack each other and we will not defend ourselves. This takes the fear out of telling each other what we are really feeling, or thinking, about a matter. If we feel we have possibly misunderstood the other, we can go back to tip number 5 and complete the communication cycle, but we do it without attacking or blaming each other.

7. *Have regular couple-communication times.* We suggest that you have a daily time when you simply touch base and share with each other. Perhaps a tea time or coffee time each morning would be a good format for a couple time. Our Marriage Encounter friends benefit from their regular times when they record their feelings and thoughts in a journal for ten minutes and then share what they have written with each other and talk about it. One couple we know cleans up the kitchen together each morning after breakfast. While it only takes a couple of minutes, it's when they touch base. Using whatever works best for you, find a way to touch emotionally each day. Your marriage will be the benefactor!

SORRY, NO SHORTCUTS!

There is no shortcut to developing interpersonal competency. It takes years to forge a deep, personal relationship and to learn to talk to each other on an intimate level, though implementing the above steps will make a real difference in your relationship right away.

So to any couple in the second half of marriage, remember: deep, intimate, personal conversations don't just happen. You make them happen through lots of hard work. It will take time and effort, but you can restore your passion for your marriage. You can have intimate conversations for two!

∾

MARRIAGE BUILDER

Expressing Positive Feelings

Since it is not easy for some to communicate feelings, begin by brainstorming positive feelings words. Then it is easier to form them into encouraging statements. Here are some words to get you started:

"I feel ..."

happy	optimistic
excited	enthusiastic
joyful	pleased
content	encouraged
relaxed	creative
grateful	calm
loved	secure
confident	

Now think about all the positive things about your mate and write them into encouraging sentences, using feelings words. (For example, "I am *relaxed* when I am in your presence" or "I feel *secure* when I am in your arms" or "I am *encouraged* when you give me your undivided attention.")

Next, look for opportunities to verbalize your positive feelings to your mate!

MARRIAGE BUILDER

Expressing Negative Feelings

Since we have difficulty communicating anger in a positive way, begin by brainstorming negative feelings words. Then it is easier to form them into statements that are helpful and do not blame or attack the other person. Here are some words to get you started:

"I feel . . ."

hurt	sad	uneasy
frustrated	trapped	embarrassed
angry	squelched	anxious
threatened	scared	belittled
lonely	afraid	used
confused	pressured	attacked
stressed	crushed	irritated
depressed	ignored	tense

Now think of a couple of situations in which you would like to be able to express your negative feelings, but express them in a positive way. Write out what you would like to say, using feelings words and without attacking or blaming your spouse.

Remember to start your sentences with "I." (For example, "I feel *anxious* when we don't talk through our budget and decide together how to spend our money" or "I feel *frustrated* when we spend most of our time talking about our children and their problems" or "I am *fearful* that we aren't adequately preparing for retirement.")

MARRIAGE BUILDER

"Can We Talk about It?"

Make a list of topics for discussion:

1. Topics I would like to talk about:

2. Topics I think my mate would like to talk about:

3. Topics I'm not ready to talk about right now. Let's wait on these:

Challenge Four

❧

*Use Anger and Conflict in a Creative Way
to Build Your Relationship*

One of the best aspects of our marriage is learning to disagree, stand our ground, and still be friends and lovers.

—husband married for thirty years

Why does my husband have to always win? He won't apologize or admit it when he's wrong. On some issues, I don't feel I'm taken very seriously, which makes me reluctant to confide my fears or opinions to him. This makes me withdraw, which adds to our lack of communication. I tend to be overly sensitive, so if he doesn't sugarcoat his responses, that further complicates matters.

—wife married for seven years, second marriage

We had the divorce papers ready to sign a couple of times a number of years ago, but both times we looked at each other and said, "But I haven't stopped loving you." Even when we couldn't agree on virtually anything else, we have always agreed on that. Nothing we've been through was bad enough to kill the love we have for each other.

—wife married for eighteen years

Our marriage is a real partnership; we both give to make our marriage work. It takes time to work things through, but that's what we're committed to doing.

—husband married for thirty-one years

In every marriage the two dynamic forces are love, which seeks to draw the couple together, and anger, which tends to drive them apart.

—David Mace[1]

Building a marriage is similar to flying a plane. Our friend Jake is a commercial pilot and always seems to have another "flying experience" to tell us—like the time he backed the plane away from the gate at Washington National Airport, cut it too close, and backed the plane into the terminal! He had to explain to the passengers why they had to disembark and change planes.

Jake loves to fly—especially when the weather is sunny and the winds are calm—but he tells us that bad weather and air turbulence are just part of flying. "In piloting a plane, conditions continually change," Jake said. "Some turbulence can be avoided, but sometimes you simply have to fly through it. The problem is, you don't know how much turbulence is out there, and you don't know how far it is to smooth air."

We asked Jake about degrees of turbulence. He answered, "There are four degrees of turbulence—light, moderate, severe, and extreme. Light turbulence is when your coffee jiggles; moderate turbulence is when the coffee spills."

He went on to explain that severe and extreme turbulence are to be avoided if at all possible. Personally, he has flown in both but has never intentionally taken passengers into severe turbulence.

Pressing him a little further, we asked what he does on those occasions when he is caught in severe turbulence. His immediate response was, "I slow down! The ride won't be pleasant, but my goal is to incur no structural damage to the plane or harm to the passengers. The rough ride isn't nearly as important as potential damage to the occupants or to the plane."

AVOID MARITAL TURBULENCE

The only way to avoid turbulence in marriage is to stay on the ground and go nowhere. There are midlife couples who would rather stay static and motionless than experience turbulence and growth. But for those in the second half of marriage who choose to build a more intimate, companionship marriage, there's an excellent chance you will experience turbulence on occasion. We usually handle the light turbulence with expertise and humor. Moderate turbulence presents a bigger challenge. It's the severe and extreme turbulence that is most difficult to handle. And at these times, we can take a tip from Jake: the goal is to preserve the relationship and incur no structural damage to our marriage!

Arps on Overload—Again!

We tend to experience turbulence when we're under stress. Our marriage plane may already be too full of things to do, and we are simply overloaded. On these occasions, even light turbulence can create discord—like the time we Arps were getting ready to fly to Grand Rapids, Michigan, to meet with the good folks at Zondervan and talk about this book.

Here's scene one: It's late at night. Our flight is early the next morning. We haven't even begun to pack. While Claudia is usually the willing packer, on this occasion she wants help from her coauthor! Good-natured Dave is the willing helper—in his own time, which isn't Claudia's preferred schedule. Can't he just get the bags from the attic?

Yes, he can and does. He even hangs up the garment bag—but in the wrong place. "Dave," Claudia complains, "you know I don't want it on our bedroom door. I always put it on the closet door."

"OK, OK!" Dave says. "You don't have to get so upset; it's no big deal. I'll move it." And in an effort to placate the packer, Dave moves the hang-up bag, scratching our bedroom door in the process. If you remember, this is our new, dream-house condo—one that until now was without a scratched bedroom door.

Claudia's frustration bubbles over onto Dave. Not a pretty picture—and we are in the process of writing this book on marriage. Claudia—who, according to Dave, often gets her exercise jumping to conclusions—is ready to cancel the book contract and forget the whole deal. Instead, she huffs and puffs and packs our bags.

Scene two: It's past our bedtime. We finally go to bed. Claudia, still perturbed, can't go to sleep, so she starts reading *Why Marriages Succeed or Fail,* a book we are using in researching this book. It is the copy on the back cover that gets her attention: "If you love your mate but your marriage seems to be off track, this book is for you."

Sometimes we are the ones who benefit the most from our own research. Claudia runs across a self-test to answer the question, "Is there enough love and respect in your marriage?"

I could use some more of that, she thinks to herself. But as she begins to take the test, her attitude changes. She reads things like:

My spouse seeks out my opinions.
My spouse cares about my feelings.
We listen to each other.
We respect each other's ideas.
There's a lot of love in our marriage.
We are very good friends.
I feel included in my partner's life.[2]

It becomes clear to Claudia how much Dave loves and respects her. As she scores him twenty out of twenty (all positive answers indicating love and respect), she realizes the insignificance of that scratch on our bedroom door. She looks over to Dave, nudges him awake, and says, "I really appreciate you!"

Completely surprised, he responds, "I appreciate you, too." Then he rolls over and goes back to sleep.

Once again, we needed to slow down and refocus on appreciating and pleasing each other. An enriched marriage is a lifetime commitment followed by daily commitments to put marriage first and personal wishes and rights second. For us that means copiloting, and together setting the course for our marriage.

As Copilots, Agree on Where You're Going

Make sure that as copilots you agree on the direction you're headed. In the second half of marriage, defined roles are fewer and the division of responsibilities is blurred. For a harmonious flight, you need to have a way to come to a consensus when there is a difference of opinion. No longer does "I'll just make the decision" work. With a companionship marriage, you can be partners in piloting your marriage.

IDENTIFYING MARITAL TURBULENCE

Constructive arguing involves expressing negative feelings in a positive way. In the last chapter, we saw that the avoider tends to suppress anger, while the confronter tends to vent it. Both need to learn to express their strong negative feelings in a way that releases positive energy and builds their relationship. It is not unlike learning to speak a new language. They have to learn how to work out their anger as a couple. Only then are couples equipped to take steps to resolve an issue. Let's look closer at how to process anger.

First Deal With Your Own Anger

"That's great," said one wife in a recent Marriage Alive seminar. "I've learned how to express my negative feelings and anger to my husband, Fred, in this way, but he just looks at me and says, 'So what?' What am I supposed to do now?"

"First, deal with your own anger," we told her. "Expressing your negative feelings without attacking your husband is a positive step. However, you may need to analyze your own feelings."

When we have negative feelings, we need to look inward before we can relate outward. Dr. Harriet Lerner, in *The Dance of Anger*, points out, "When emotional intensity is high, many of us engage in nonproductive efforts to change the other person, and in so doing, fail to exercise our power to clarify and change our own selves." She suggests several questions to ask yourself:

What am I really angry about?

What is the problem and whose problem is it?

How can I sort out who is responsible for what?

How can I learn to express my anger in a way that will not leave me feeling helpless and powerless?

When I am angry, how can I clearly communicate my position without becoming defensive or attacking?

What risks and losses might I face if I become clearer and more assertive?[3]

When dealing with our own anger, remember that, as we stated in challenge 1, we can change no other person by direct action. We can only change ourselves. But an interesting thing happens—when we change our responses, others may change in response to us. Dr. Lerner notes,

> We are responsible for our own behavior. But we are not responsible for other people's reactions; nor are they responsible for ours. . . . We begin to use our anger as a vehicle for change when we are able to share our reactions without holding the other person responsible for causing our feelings, and without blaming ourselves for the reactions that other people have in response to our choices and actions.[4]

Processing Anger as a Couple

Once we are aware of our own negative feelings and have some understanding of them, we are ready to confront anger as a couple. We will always be indebted to our mentors, David and Vera Mace, for helping us to handle anger as a couple and to use it as a positive force in our relationship. The Maces suggest that a couple make an anger contract. The greatest problem in marriage is not the lack of communication but the inability to handle and process anger. Anger is a normal, healthy emotion; a person who doesn't get angry is not a normal human being. However, once angry, we are responsible for what we do. Venting anger simply increases the intensity, and suppressing anger is unhealthy. The Maces suggest that a better way is to process anger.

They made a contract that they activate at the first sign of anger. Here are their three steps, which we've modified and adopted as our own:

1. We agree to acknowledge our anger to each other as soon as we become aware of it.
2. We renounce the right to vent anger at each other. It's OK to say something like, "I'm getting angry with you, but you know I'm not going to attack you." The other person does not have to defend himself. (Remember our agreement in the last chapter that we will not attack each other or defend ourselves? This step reinforces that commitment.)
3. We will each ask for the other's help in dealing with anger that develops. If your partner is angry with you and appeals to you to help clear it up, it is very much in your interest to respond. The Maces suggest forming a coalition. They say, "Our contract commits us to working on each angry situation that develops between us until we clear it up."[5]

We have included a copy of our anger contract for your own personal use at the end of this chapter.

RESOLVING MARITAL TURBULENCE

No one does it all right; the Arps are no exception. The time Dave scratched our door with the clothes bag, Claudia totally forgot we even had an anger contract! But we do remember it most of the time, and that's what makes the difference.

The reason it is important to deal with angry feelings is that in most conflicts, it isn't the facts that are bothering us, it's the strong negative feelings. Once those feelings are diffused and processed, it's simple to work at resolving the conflict. And you don't have to agree on everything. If we agreed on everything, one of us would be unnecessary!

Steps for Resolving Conflict

There are a number of problem-solving formulas, but most contain four steps:

1. State the problem. Too often couples try to resolve conflict without agreeing on what the conflict really is! We find it helpful to write it out so that we're both trying to resolve the same thing.

2. Identify what is at stake and what each has invested. Who has the greatest need for a solution? When Claudia was less satisfied than Dave about the division of labor in our home, Claudia felt the greatest need for a solution!

3. List possible solutions. The more the merrier. We brainstorm and think of as many solutions as possible. And remember, adding humor will relieve stress and lighten up any situation.

4. Choose one and try it! If your first choice doesn't work, don't give up. Check your list and try another possible solution and then another until something works. Over the years as we have searched for solutions for our own issues and have helped other couples work through theirs, a pattern seemed to develop. Most issues are resolved in one of three ways.

The first way is to give a gift of love. We ask if whatever we are talking about is more important to one than to the other. Then the one to whom it is less important may simply agree to give in and give a gift of love. The Scriptures tell us it is more blessed to give than to receive, and this is certainly true in marriage—unless it's one person who is doing all of the giving, and then you have another problem!

The second way to find resolution is to compromise—for each to give a little; to meet somewhere in the middle. Many times we compromise. There are other times when we simply agree to disagree, and that's the third way to settle an issue. Some things aren't that important, and as we said, we don't need to agree on everything. We agree with Ray Ortlund: "Why do we have to agree, or win, or conclude every discussion? Some great truths are opposites and must forever be held in tension."[6]

At times we like to debate. (Let's clarify that: Claudia likes to debate. For Dave, debating with Claudia is a gift of love.) It can be intellectually stimulating to have differing views. A little turbulence can be healthy for the second half of marriage.

Constructive Arguing Can Enrich Your Marriage

Constructive arguments can actually enrich your marriage, and research proves it. According to a recent study of 156 middle-aged and older couples, a major feature of long-lasting marriages is the ability of spouses to argue constructively. "But happily married couples argue quite differently from unhappy couples," says researcher Dr. Laura Carstensen. "Both types express anger but do so in distinct ways."[7]

When healthy couples argue, Carstensen says, they stay focused on the issue, not on name-calling. They defuse anger with signs of affection—a loving word, a tender touch, a warm gesture, and they use humor in a positive way. "They laugh with each other, not at each other," says Carstensen. "Humor helps keep love alive." The study indicates that with age, old wars become less important and marital bonds are strengthened![8]

Humor has come to our rescue more than once—like the morning after Claudia's little "packing the bags for our trip" episode: As we were leaving for the airport to catch our early-morning flight, we were exhausted. Claudia smiled at Dave and said, "My, isn't this glamorous? Are we having fun yet? This must be the lifestyle of the rich and famous!"

"You've got to be kidding!" responded Dave. Claudia was.

So let us encourage you to let anger, conflict, and humor enrich your relationship. One of these days, it may save your life—it did ours!

A Mountaintop Experience

Soon after we signed our anger contract, we had an opportunity to put it to good use. It literally saved our lives. Several years back, after a stressful summer of writing deadlines, we slipped away to the Swiss Alps. When our children were growing up in Europe, one of our favorite family places was Engelberg, Switzerland, a little alpine village far away from the tourist traffic. So we went back to Engelberg. On our first day, we decided to hike where we had hiked years ago with our three sons. The lovely sloping path, vivid in our memories, would be just right for our first day of hiking.

A cable car had replaced the cogged railroad we had taken with our boys. No problem—that is, until we had to choose where to get off. Claudia felt that the first stop was it. Dave's response was, "No way. We haven't gone far enough!" The cable car took us still higher. The terrain became more rugged, and the steep cliffs below did not look inviting to us fair-weather hikers. At the next stop, we got off and looked for the easy way down. We realized we were not where we'd planned to be!

Thinking we had found an easy path, we began our descent. The path was sloping and wonderful—for the first thirty minutes. Then suddenly it became steep and rugged. Looking for an easier way down, we got off the path and ended up at a precipice. The jagged rocks gave a rough appearance to the sheer drop-off. It was scary! We were lost in the Alps, but we weren't alone; anger was right there with us. Fortunately, on that day we remembered our anger contract.

"Dave," Claudia began, "I'm getting angry with you, but I'm not going to attack you." Dave, relieved, took a few steps back from the cliff, just in case she changed her mind. Claudia continued, saying, "We should have got off at the first stop. I'm frightened and it looks as if it could rain at any moment! How are we going to get off this mountain without breaking a leg?"

Dave, also concerned, agreed we had definitely made a mistake. He too was concerned. But because we didn't let our anger win, we could still think logically and attack the problem (that is, "How do we get off the mountain?") and not each other. On that day, our anger contract worked well! Slowly we began to retrace our steps and eventually found the path. The trip down was challenging; we needed all our concentration as a team to stay on the path and find our way. A couple of hours later we actually found the path we had taken years ago. The sun reappeared. And because of our anger contract, we were still friends; we were able to enjoy the path! The next day, our muscles were sore and we couldn't move, but that's another story!

We encourage you to practice processing anger and resolving conflict. Put these skills to work in your marriage. They can help make the rest of your marriage the best, and someday they may save your life. We wouldn't climb the Alps without them!

WHY MARRIAGE TURBULENCE IS HEALTHY

Thinking differently gives texture to a long-term marriage. In a healthy marriage, it's safe to disagree and get angry. A healthy marriage is a safe place to resolve honest conflict and process your anger. It can help your marriage grow. In *The Good Marriage*, Dr. Wallerstein reminds us,

> A good marriage provides a holding environment for aggression. Broadly speaking, the couple's love and friendship, the togetherness they have built, their shared interest and history, including the children, all combine to provide the overall structure that contains the aggression. The ties that unite them are far stronger than the forces that divide them.[9]

A long-term marriage has too much history to throw it away. Especially when it can get better—even when you disagree! Now it's time for you to examine your own marital skies—to look at how you really feel, how you can begin to process anger through signing and using an anger contract, and how you can resolve conflict in a way that turns your marital turbulence into a smooth flight. Take our challenge and you'll discover that you can fly the friendly skies with your copilot! Have a great trip!

———————— ❧ ————————

MARRIAGE BUILDER

Dealing With Marital Turbulence

You can do this exercise alone or as a couple. If you are doing it alone, first go through the list of questions and answer them for yourself. Then go through it a second time and answer them the way you think your spouse would answer. Seek to see things from his or her perspective, and it can benefit your relationship.

Part One: Identifying Areas of Marital Turbulence

List possible areas:

Rate each area: light, moderate, severe, extreme

Part Two: Identifying My Style

I usually resolve conflict by:

___giving gifts of love

___giving a little to find a solution

___agreeing to disagree

___other

What I would like to do in the future:

Part Three: Is There Presently an Issue That Needs to Be Resolved?

Can I express my negative feelings in a positive way, without blaming or attacking?

Is there some way I can diffuse the anger?

Is there a way to resolve the issue?

___give gift of love

___compromise

___agree to disagree

MARRIAGE BUILDER

Processing Our Anger

Consider the following questions. If possible, discuss with your mate.

How do you currently handle anger?

How would you like to handle anger?

Are you willing to sign the anger contract?

———————— ✎ ————————

MARRIAGE BUILDER

Anger Contract

The following can become your own anger contract. Trust us, this is one of the most important contracts you will ever sign.

✎

Whenever one of us becomes angry,

1. we will acknowledge our anger to each other as soon as we become aware of it;
2. we will renounce the right to vent anger at each other or to defend ourselves;
3. we will ask for each other's help in dealing with the anger that has developed.[10]

Signed   _____

Signed   _____

Challenge Five

*Build a Deeper Friendship and
Enjoy Your Spouse*

---— ✣ ---—

*My advice to those entering the second half of marriage is to find
things you can do together to build your friendship. These things
will be even more rewarding as time goes by.*

—husband married for forty-one years

*Ask the question, "Who is my best friend?" If it is your mate,
there will be no problem with the empty nest.*

—husband married for thirty-two years

*This year has been a time of growth for us as a couple.
It started with lots of stress—overcommitment and relationship
problems—but God helped us through it. We just celebrated
our twentieth anniversary with a romantic getaway. We've become
best friends again. Hope can be restored!*

—wife married for twenty years

*One of the best things about our marriage is our adventuresome
spirit. We are best friends, like to try new things, and laugh a lot!*

—wife married for twenty-seven years

———— ✿ ————

In survey after survey, at least 80 percent of couples in successful long-term relationships report that they have become best friends. . . . They feel accepted with their faults and have come to accept their mates as a package deal.

—Dr. Georgia Witkin[1]

Getting to airports on time reveals one of our differences and—from time to time—the depth of our friendship. Dave's ideal scenario is to arrive at the airport just in time to check bags, park the car, and walk down the jetway to board the plane—forget wasting time sitting at the gate, waiting for the flight to be called!

Claudia prefers a much more leisurely pace. She likes to get to the airport early—really early. Her motto is, "We've never missed a plane by being too early." She likes to have time for a cup of coffee and prefers to get the best seat at the gate.

Well, on this particular day, we were on Dave's preferred timetable, so we decided to divide and conquer. Not only were we running late but we needed to exchange frequent flyer coupons for tickets for our ski getaway the next week at Crested Butte in the Colorado Rockies. This was our treat to each other for surviving a very hectic fall, and it was an opportunity to shore up our friendship. One more business trip and then it would be fun, fun, fun! We could already hear our skis swish!

Dave dropped Claudia off at the curb. His job was to check bags and park the car. Claudia's assignment was to drop our bills in the mail and exchange the coupons for tickets for our upcoming getaway.

Sounds simple but it got complicated fast. As Claudia was mailing the bills, she also mailed the coupons!

When Dave entered the airport, there was Claudia at the Delta counter, saying tearfully, "Dave, I mailed our coupons. We can't get our tickets for Colorado, because the coupons are in that mailbox right over there!"

So what did we do? There are times when you are either going to laugh or cry. Claudia's choice was obvious. Dave's reaction wasn't laughter, but he smiled and said, "Hey, it's OK. I could have done the same thing. We'll work it out." It helps that he is the eternal optimist.

The Delta agent, observing us, came to our rescue. He gave us the phone numbers to call in order to start the complicated process of replacing our coupons so we could get our tickets issued. As we went through our week of meetings, Claudia told our coupon story time and time again. Each time, she laughed at her humanity a little bit more. And after a number of phone calls and express-mail letters, Delta replaced the coupons and salvaged our ski getaway.

THE FRIENDSHIP FACTOR

Maybe you've never mailed your plane tickets, but perhaps you've tested your friendship in other ways. Daily we prove we are not perfect. Relaxing and giving ourselves and each other permission to make mistakes helps us build our friendship and maintain a sense of humor. It ultimately adds fun to our marriage. And friendship and fun in marriage—especially in the second half—is important. Have you ever seen a couple on the way to the divorce court who were best friends and having fun together?

What are you doing to build your friendship with your spouse? In this chapter, we want to look at ways we can build our friendship and have fun together. Also, we'll address an important part of friendship in the second half of marriage: taking care of our health and pacing ourselves for the second half. Finally, you will meet Lucy and William, who have been married for over fifty years and have managed to meet this challenge with vim and vigor!

GETTING STARTED

An important part of friendship in the second half of marriage is simply spending time together. Remember, a companionship marriage is one in which you put the other person first and your marriage before both of you. That assumes you are spending time together. Daily we have the opportunity to encourage each other and to build our friendship. But we must be intentional about it!

According to psychologists Richard Matterson and Janis Long Harris, "the key to a stronger friendship—and a more satisfying marriage—is developing new habits."[2] What new habits would you like to develop with your mate? How can you stretch your present friendship boundaries?

Matterson and Harris also point out that we have different friendship styles: "Men value *doing* things together, while women value *talking* together. For that reason, shared activities and regular times to talk go hand in hand, allowing the friendship needs of each spouse to be met."[3]

JUST FOR FUN

From our survey and our Marriage Alive seminar participants, we gathered information on what couples who are best friends are doing for fun. Here are some of their responses (note that all contain the two required elements of talking and doing):

> *"We like to take the back roads, get lost, and then find our way home again."*
>
> *"We like to cook together. Lately, we've been learning to cook Chinese."*
>
> *"We pick berries together."*
>
> *"We do organic gardening."*
>
> *"We learned to sail together."*
>
> *"We enjoy keeping our grandchildren—one child at a time."*
>
> *"On Saturday morning we have a standing date to run errands together."*
>
> *"We like to rock in our double rocker on our screened porch."*

"One night we slept out on our balcony under the stars."

"Occasionally we like to drive instead of fly for long trips."

"We like to read aloud together."

"When we miss our grandchildren, we borrow small children for an evening."

"From time to time we like to pull out the family albums, slides, videos, and reminisce."

"On our twenty-fifth wedding anniversary, we made a list of twenty-five things we wanted to do. Then we did them!"

"We've recently learned how to use E-mail and now stay in better contact with our children."

Make your own fun list of things you can do that include both talking and activity. For a guide, use the Marriage Builder at the end of this chapter.

BUT MY BACK HURTS!

Building a long-term friendship is much easier if it can be experienced with the backdrop of a healthy body. It is definitely easier to maintain that friendship when we also maintain our health.

From our survey, by far the greatest fears that spouses have for the future were related to health concerns—either for themselves or their spouse. Of those in the survey ages fifty and over, 59 percent said that the thing they feared most was death and/or illness, compared with only 19.5 percent of those under fifty.

Many of us find the approach of the second half of life particularly disorienting. Some have a negative attitude, like the husband who said, "Just around the corner, I'm going to lose my hair, my hearing will go, then my eyes, and my sex drive, and then I'll just roll over and die."

Wait a minute! Life doesn't have to be so negative, especially if we take care of ourselves. Why is it that around midlife, our eyesight, backs, and hearing start to go? Shouldn't the extra pounds we gain help fortify us with good health? But the opposite seems to be true. Since health and lifestyle issues are so important to our marriage in the second half, here are six tips that are helping us to live a more balanced and healthy life.

Tips for Making the Second Half More Enjoyable

1. Take care of yourself. Investments in your health are investments in your friendship with your spouse. "If I had known I was going to live so long," a friend told us, "I would have taken better care of myself!"

A few years ago our backs gave us a midlife wake-up call. Up to that point, we had abused our backs. One day Claudia's back said, "No more!" She had ignored the warning signs. Then, a couple of weeks after our second son's wedding, as she was walking down the stairs her back simply signaled to her, "Honey, you're not going anywhere!" Three weeks later she began to function again, but it was a long trip back to the land of healthy backs. Along the way, she learned the importance of taking care of herself. Physical therapy, exercise, and fitness walking became a way of life. When she takes care of herself, her back does fine. When she doesn't take care of herself, her back hurts. It's as simple as that.

How long has it been since you've had a physical? When have you taken a hard look at your diet? Are you getting the exercise you need? If you want to enjoy the second half of life, take our advice: take care of yourself; if you don't, no one else will!

2. Pace yourself. We are learning to pace ourselves. We simply can't go at the pace we went ten years ago. We've made some basic decisions, like no early-morning appointments if we can help it. We try to limit "multipurpose" trips. Of course, we make an exception to stop by and see grandchildren! We aren't as quick to say, "No problem. Of course we can do it!" What changes do you need to make in order to pace yourself?

3. Build relationships and maintain them. Beef up friendships for this time of life. Don't look to extended family for all of your fun. Make friends with other couples. Family is more fun when you don't have expectations. Maintain a support system. When our children were adolescents, our own social life went down the drain. Like during the toddler years, we were "on call" most nights, and with our sons' activities, there was little time left over. Forget time for friends! So over the past few years, we've worked to rebuild old friendships and establish new ones.

4. Stretch your boundaries. The second half of marriage is a great time to stretch boundaries by trying new things. Soon after our last son left the nest, we decided to cash in some of our frequent flyer points for a summer vacation in Europe. Usually we traveled to Europe in the winter, when the rates are cheap, so we decided to relish this new adventure. Claudia got our tickets in December and put them under our Christmas tree as our gift to us. That Christmas, our friends John and Sarah McCracken were over one evening for dinner and asked us what trips we had planned for the new year. We told them about the airline tickets under our tree, and before the evening was over, they decided to go to Europe with us! We had never traveled with friends, and we knew that our two-week vacation with John and Sarah would stretch our boundaries. Later we discovered that it would stretch theirs as well!

The first thing we discovered was our different approach to travel. We are the spontaneous, adventuresome type. Our idea of having a fixed schedule is deciding which country we will sleep in tonight. Sarah and John's idea of being flexible is to have confirmed reservations weeks ahead in a hotel where you have never stayed! Also, the McCrackens' idea of "roughing it" was on the expense level of an Arp "splurge." Talk about compromise; we experienced it firsthand with our friends. While there were some really interesting moments, both couples say it was a fantastic trip and one that deepened our friendship.

Years later it's really fun to reminisce with the McCrackens about our European vacation. Sarah still says it was the most unstructured trip of their life, while we say that never have we had so many details worked out beforehand! What will stretch your friendship boundaries? Trust us, stretching your boundaries will broaden your life! Now we're talking to the McCrackens about going to Ireland together.

A husband who had been married for thirty-four years and who participated in our survey shared some of the creative things he and his wife were doing to stretch their boundaries: "We've been trying to find things that we both enjoy and can do together. We are now playing bridge on Monday evenings. Also, we sing together at a nursing home on Wednesday nights. We are beginning to record songs together just for fun. I can see how people who don't want to stretch their boundaries could have difficulty at this stage of marriage, but we're both eager to help each other. I find it a very nice time of life!"

5. *Stay involved with life.* We are better friends to each other when we are involved with life. Be active. Find your passion. Continue to learn and grow. Look for ways to be creative. Lester and Rose were both chemists and had a knack for experimenting with life. Life at their home was never boring. As their children were growing up, they chose to live in downtown New York City. They traveled extensively with their children and gave them the rich heritage of being world citizens. When the children left home, Lester and Rose's dwelling could be best described as the "creative nest"! In retirement, they decided to learn Russian. Who knows what they will do next! Be willing to take risks. Try different things. Life may be many things, but it won't be boring.

6. *Hang in there.* When you're discouraged, don't throw your life away. Don't throw away at fifty what you'll want at sixty. Don't make a major decision or drastic changes when you're down. Maintain some traditions and start some new ones. We remember one of the first Christmases after we entered the empty nest, when we simply adapted too much. In an attempt to accommodate our adult children and their spouses, we gave up too much that was precious and meaningful to us.

For instance, everyone wanted to go to a different Christmas Eve service. By the time we made a decision, it was too late and we missed going to one. So the next year, we announced which service we two were going to attend, invited anyone who wanted to go with us to come along, and let everyone make their own plans. Over the years, we have found what is comfortable for us.

Life is a series of adjustments. Changes are as certain as the seasons. So embrace change. Greet it as a welcome guest. If you don't like the way things are right now, don't panic—more changes may be just up the road! Grab the initiative and do what you can do to put more fun into your life and more life into your friendship with your spouse. You can start anytime, and it can start with you!

LUCY AND WILLIAM

Recently an old friend reminded us that it takes one heart and one initiator to spice up friendship in a long-term marriage. As we boarded our flight to Atlanta, we were surprised to see Lucy. Since there was an empty seat in our row, Lucy joined us. For the entire flight, we talked about her fifty-year-plus marriage. Lucy was flying to her son's home in California to meet her husband, William, who was returning from Asia, where he had been speaking. William is a retired pastor who really has never retired. His passion is missions, and he still speaks all over the world, plus is an interim pastor in a church. Lucy said that working together as a team in the ministry helped prepare them for the time their children left home. "I didn't fall apart," she said, "and one reason was, we had built our marriage and ministered together." Coming from a very traditional marriage, she sure had some modern ideas for making it work. Here are some of her jewels:

"We have dates as often as we can. We have done this for years! We really enjoy going out to eat with each other. But when our finances and time were limited, I'd pack a picnic lunch, go to William's office, and pick him up. We'd go to a park when the weather was nice. Sometimes we just had our picnic in the car. I'd get him back to the office in time for his afternoon appointments.

"Other things we like to do together are going to concerts, the opera, and plays. Recently William took me to Atlanta to see *Miss Saigon*. We like to travel together—like taking a cruise—which I usually have to initiate, but that's OK with me.

"William has always traveled. I still don't let him leave home without a love note in the pajama pocket. I also put notes in his briefcase. I always want to have the last word from home!

"I also travel and speak at conferences. [That's what she had been doing that weekend.] So wherever we are, when we are apart we call each other every evening. I get kidded about this all the time, with comments like: 'Lucy, has William called yet?' 'Better go on to your room, you'll miss William's call.' People kid me but I think they are envious. After over fifty years of marriage, how many people call each other each night when they are apart? But one night this past weekend, there was no call from William, and my friends really got worried. Then I discovered they had sent the message to the wrong room. I've always called William during the day, just to say hello and that I'm thinking about him. Some say men are not as sentimental, but I know William likes the little things I do.

"I send him cards even when we aren't traveling, just to express my love and appreciation. If the cards don't say exactly what I'm feeling, I just edit them.

"I make William's favorite date cookies, and when he is coming home from a trip, I delight in cooking his favorite meal—scalloped potatoes, meat loaf, green beans, tomato aspic salad, and apple pie. Around the holidays, I always make him a pumpkin pie, and he knows it's a gift of love, because I don't like it and he gets to eat it all!"

"What makes your marriage work besides all the fun?" we asked her.

"I can think of two things," she replied. "First, don't ever put your spouse down in public. If you have a suggestion to make, save it for when you are alone. Second, don't ever go to bed angry. We kneel, hold hands, and pray together when we go to bed at night. It's hard to do that and remain angry. I don't know why it is so hard for couples to pray together, but over the years, it's been the glue that helped us keep it all together."

As we reflected on our conversation with Lucy, we realized that praying together and dating your mate have more in common than one would think. We close this chapter with ten dating suggestions for the second half of marriage.

Ten Fun Dates

1. Formal-dinner-in-the-park date. Put on your black tie and evening gown and grab the picnic basket for an evening under the stars!

2. I'm-just-too-tired date. Order takeout, turn on the answering machine, and just relax and enjoy snuggling while you read or watch a movie.

3. Photo date. Go to your favorite haunt and snap away. Simply set the timer on your camera and run back and smile!

4. Gourmet-cooking date. If you ever wanted to take up gourmet cooking, do it together and call it a date! Plan the menu, grocery shop together at an upscale market with sample gourmet coffee, and together cook your dinner!

5. Yellow-road-blue-highways date. Choose a fifty-mile radius around your home and see what you can discover. No fast foods or four-lane roads allowed!

6. Workout date. Get in shape together at a health club. Or if your budget is tight, walk or jog together.

7. Home Depot date. Go to Home Depot and dream about home improvement projects you would like to tackle or have done someday!

8. Window-shopping date. Go when the stores are closed, and it will be a cheap date! Instead of dreaming about what you would like to have, pick out all the things in the window you already have. (This could also be called the "grateful date.")

9. Airport date. Go to the airport and watch people come and go. Pretend you are saying good-bye to each other and hug and kiss passionately! Then pretend you are meeting each other after a long absence!

10. Proposal date. Go to a public place and ask your mate to marry you all over again![4]

It's now your turn for fun. What are you doing to build your friendship? What do you do just for fun? Remember, friendship and fun in marriage *is* serious business!

MARRIAGE BUILDER

Just for Fun

Make a list of things you would like to do just for fun with your mate:

1.
2.
3.
4.
5.

If you both make a list, you can combine your lists. Then choose things you want to do, in order of priority. Write them into your planner or calendar.

Memory Joggers:

1. What things do I enjoy doing with my spouse?

2. What did we enjoy doing together in the past?

3. Which of those previous activities would I still like to do?

4. What would I like for us to do together in the future?

∾

MARRIAGE BUILDER

Planning a Getaway for Two

1. Brainstorm places you would like to go (make a list and then choose one).

2. Choose possible dates available (choose one and write it down on your calendar; you also may want to choose an alternate date).

3. Designate resources for this weekend (work out a budget; decide if this will be an economy getaway or the big splurge).

4. Make arrangements (pet care, reservations, getting maps, and so on).

5. Make a packing list (don't forget to take along a CD player, candles, matches, reading material, snacks, and so forth).

6. You may want to choose a couple of subjects you would like to talk about.

7. On your way, you may want to take this husband's suggestion: "For entertainment and to stimulate discussion, on long car trips my wife and I like to listen to books-on-tape (Christian speakers, fiction, nonfiction). There's a lot available to buy, and I think you can borrow them inexpensively, if not for free, from most public libraries. It always gets us talking, and time flies!"

For a more detailed guide for a weekend getaway, see our book *The Ultimate Marriage Builder,* from which this planning guide is adapted.[5]

Challenge Six

❧

Renew Romance and Restore a Pleasurable
Sexual Relationship

The one thing I'm looking forward to in my marriage is falling in love again—hopefully soon!

—wife married for twenty years

I set our table for two with fresh flowers and just as nice as if we had someone special coming to eat with us.

—wife married for fourteen years, second marriage

The one thing I fear the most in the future is lack of sexual fulfillment for both of us.

—husband married for nineteen years

The best part of my marriage is our times of intimacy.

—wife married for forty-five years

No matter who visits us, we never give up our bed. Our bedroom is our refuge, our haven, our private resort. We protect our "marriage bed" and hopefully set an example for others.

—wife married for thirteen years, second marriage

*I thought the fire was out in my fireplace. I stirred the ashes, and
I burned my hands.*

—Antonio Machado[1]

Our most favorite getaway place in the whole world is a little chalet in the Austrian Alps. That's where we are as we write this chapter. Sometimes we come with no agenda. It's a great place to relax, and in the summer and autumn we take long walks. In the winter, we ski when we have the energy. It's wintertime now. We're not skiing. We're writing. But it helps that we are snowed in. One thing we love about this chalet is the wonderful open fireplace. It has lit our fires more than once. But we're here to work—to write this book. Of course, we do have to work on this chapter on love, and what's a chapter without a little research?

Back to our fireplace. It is rather small and the wood burns fast, so we usually burn one log at a time and watch it like a hawk. Yesterday when Dave lit the fire, the log he chose was too long to fit, so he turned it perpendicular to the fireplace and lit it. A bit later Claudia saw the log hanging out of the fireplace and rearranged it so it would continue to burn. Since it had burned for a while, it fit snugly in the fireplace the right way.

Dave walked back into the room, looked at the fire, and said, "Wow! Look how that log moved!"

Logs don't move on their own; if a fire is to keep going, someone has to stoke it. The same is true in our love life—especially in the second half of marriage. If you have a great love life, it's because you fan the flames and stoke the fire! It takes effort, but it gets chilly in a long-term marriage if the coals of passion and love have gone out! We know—from time to time our fires have burned uncomfortably low.

It usually happens when we are on overload, like the time we were in Toronto, Canada. It started with a call from one of our publishers, asking if we would be willing to do media interviews while we were in Chicago leading our Marriage Alive seminar. What would authors say but, "Yes, we'd love to"?

Another publisher called and wanted us to tack a day of meetings on the front of our trip. They were only a short distance from Chicago. "Sure," we said. "That makes sense." Then the other publisher called back. They had a great opportunity for us to do several TV programs after the ones in Chicago. It would just require a short flight to Toronto. Our aim is to please, so we said, "Of course we can do that—no problem."

The extra day we had in Chicago between all these varied activities, we used to do some footwork for our youngest son's impending wedding in Wheaton.

Why do plans sound so good before we live them? Unfortunately, this plan was a killer—and the victim was our love life. Oh, we had good meetings, a great Marriage Alive seminar, and media interviews that all seemed to go well. We found a wonderful place for the wedding rehearsal dinner. At the end of that six-day marathon, we were exhausted but thought we were over the hump. So that night we went out to celebrate.

Claudia, the day lark, needed toothpicks to hold her eyes open, but right in the middle of dinner, Dave, who doesn't always choose the best moments, commented to Claudia, "Now that we are beyond this rush of interviews, we need to work on our love life. Lately we seem to be ignoring that part of our marriage, and I'm concerned."

Claudia, who'd had one more interview than Dave that day, broke into tears. Surely this wasn't happening to the "marriage doctors" who wrote *The Love Book*! Wasn't this the empty nest we'd waited and planned for? Time for each other, time for loving. And why couldn't Dave understand how completely tired Claudia was? Why was he bringing this up? The night was ruined.

Both of us were shocked at our behavior. It was a wake-up call! We loved each other and we loved making love. Yet our schedule was crowding out our intimate times together. What could we do to change this scenario? We had no instant answers, but we had a commitment to each other to find some.

Later that spring, we were on assignment in Vienna, Austria, for three months. We used this time to work on getting control of our life. You don't fix in one day what has taken years to create. And it was more than our love life that needed repairing. We needed to retool our lifestyle and find time for healthy living and for us. We were enthusiastic about the second half of our marriage, and we wanted to be healthy enough to enjoy it.

During our three months in Europe, we slowed down and found more time for each other, and we rediscovered some simple principles for building a creative love life—principles that, frankly, we had been too busy to personally apply. We also did some reading to better understand how our bodies change over the years and how this affects our lovemaking. Following are some of our discoveries.

LOVE AND INTIMACY

One of the hardest parts of staying in love and growing closer together is learning how to keep intimacy alive through the years of a marriage—especially the second half. So says Georgia Witkin, Ph.D., clinical professor of psychiatry at Mount Sinai School of Medicine in New York and author of *Passions*. She claims to know the secret of couples who succeed: "It's their stubborn determination to stay sexually and emotionally intimate with one another through changes and challenges."[2]

Love and intimacy in a marriage grow by stages, but if we ignore our sexual relationship at any stage, it can shut down. Remember your honeymoon and your marriage before children arrived? We were novices and had so much to learn about each other. About the time things began to click for us sexually, the children started arriving, and the next marital task was to find the time and overcome eternal tiredness while parenting those little ones.

In the second decade of marriage, the big enemy is boredom. The third decade, Dr. Witkin warns, can be the dangerous years. Women tend to become more interested in sex, while men become more vulnerable. This is a time to watch out for affairs. But the good news is that if you make it through the third decade, the fourth decade of love can be a renewing time. A fulfilling and enjoyable love life can add much pleasure to the retirement years.

The key is to develop emotional intimacy, according to Dr. Witkin. As Thomas Oden said, "Sexual intimacy without interpersonal intimacy is like a diploma without an education."

Researcher Judith Wallerstein gives more good news. She reports,

> It is commonly believed that sexual activity is at its height during the early years of marriage. But that was not always true for the couples in the study. Nor did sexual activity necessarily decline over the years. In many marriages high activity in the early years was followed by a decline when the children were young and then a strong rise after the children left home, continuing into the retirement years.[3]

This correlates with the discoveries from our survey.

Stressing the importance of a healthy sexual relationship in long-term marriages, Wallerstein states in her book *The Good Marriage*,

> It is very important for all couples to find ways to protect their privacy, to cherish their sexual relationship, and to guard it fiercely. A richly rewarding and stable sex life is not just a fringe benefit, it is the central task of marriage. In a good marriage, sex and love are inseparable. Sex serves a very serious function in maintaining both the quality and the stability of the relationship, replenishing emotional reserves, and strengthening the marital bond.[4]

If sex is that important to a good marriage, we need to reexamine our attitude toward sex. We need to learn what we can expect from our bodies at this stage, and discover what we can do to enhance our love life as we age.

ATTITUDE CHECKUP

In our American culture, sexuality—particularly in married life—has been a sensitive issue. And in the Christian culture, for centuries the attitude was to avoid discussing sex. Only in recent years has this begun to change. Now sex is talked about and written about in many books and magazines. (We've written a few of those articles.) But it is still difficult for most marrieds to say the "S" word. However, if we don't talk about it, we won't be able to change our attitude and develop intimacy.

The picture from media is no help. To know that our culture is interested in sex only requires that you turn on the TV and watch a few programs and commercials. Sex is used to sell everything from dishwasher liquid to batteries. But don't look to the media for healthy models of married love! Even if you occasionally find one, it most likely will not be a couple in the second half of life. The idea of sex as having any significance for elderly couples has been basically ignored in the media.

Have you heard the frog joke that seems to say that older men aren't interested in sex? We heard it twice in the last month! An older man walking down the road heard a frog talking. "If you pick me up and kiss me," said the frog, "I'll turn into a beautiful woman." The man picked up the frog and put it in his pocket. The frog complained, "Aren't you going to kiss me? I'll turn into a really sexy woman, and you can take me home with you."

The man responded, "Frankly, I'd rather have a talking frog!"

David and Vera Mace observed a tendency for people not to associate sexuality with older people at all but rather to assume that as people grow old, they gradually lose interest in sex, just as they do in many other youthful pursuits. The result of this tendency is that little serious research has been done on sex and aging. But this is changing.

The Maces report some interesting trends in their book *Letters to a Retired Couple*. They note that while the frequency of intercourse does gradually decrease over the years, sexual activity certainly plays a part in many older marriages, and that researchers report renewal of interest at quite late ages. As expected, there is a relationship between general health and sexual activity. Another study emphasized that sexual activity tends to enhance the health and happiness of the marriage partners. The Maces write,

> At the same time, there was evidence that a general state of happiness in marriage is not as dependent on an active sex life as is commonly supposed. A study concluded that when sexual intercourse cannot be continued, a loving couple tend to compensate by "emotional intimacy, sitting and lying close to each other, touching, and holding hands."
>
> What seems very clear, for older couples as well as the younger ones, is that the sex relationship is not, as some people have been suggesting, a matter of *performance*. Much more, it is a function of the interpersonal quality of the couple's relationship and must be judged in that perspective. Clearly, some older couples continue to enjoy their sex life as the years pass, while others reduce its frequency or have to give it up altogether as their general health and vigor deteriorate. What really matters is that good sex is the expression of a warm and close love relationship. If that relationship exists, its continuity is not seriously disturbed when the sexual aspect can no longer continue.[5]

If the Maces are right, then attitude is key to a fulfilled sexual relationship in the second half of marriage. We can begin to change our attitude and be more comfortable discussing the sexual side of marriage when we understand how our bodies change as we age.

HOW OUR BODIES CHANGE

The best and most practical information about how our bodies change—and how sex changes—as we get older was in the form of a short article written by Edwin Kiester Jr. and Sally Valente Kiester.[6]

Both men and women undergo normal physical, psychological, and hormonal changes. Menopause in women is a well-known stage of life, but it is less known that men also go through hormonal changes. This has been tagged "male menopause." These changes may affect interest in, and desire for, sex. However, none of these changes should interfere with a satisfying sex life. If we recognize and understand these changes, we can even improve our sex lives.

As women age, the vaginal tissues become thinner, drier, and slower to lubricate. And as a result of reduced blood flow, a middle-aged man's erection may not be as firm as when he was young. For the wife, the solution may be as simple as using an over-the-counter, water-soluble lubricant such as K-Y Jelly. And for the husband, the solution may simply be to realize that a softer erection will not prevent him from reaching orgasm. Experts say that these changes can actually enhance your sexual relationship if you discover ways to capitalize on them. Kiester and Kiester give the following five suggestions:

Enhancing Your Love Life for the Second Half

1. Reset the pace. The sexual relationship can be more satisfying in your fifties than it was in your twenties, if you reset the pace. According to a 1994 University of Chicago study, women in their twenties are least likely to achieve orgasm during intercourse. Women in their early forties are most likely! One reason for this is that a man's response time slows down as he ages. And if he is wise, he learns that by concentrating on how he can increase his wife's pleasure, he can increase his own pleasure as well.

So if your response time has slowed down, relax and enjoy it! Think of sex in the second half of marriage as a delightful stroll—not a sprint. Take it slower and savor the experience.

2. Take action. Why do so many tired wives who aren't in the mood for loving get undressed in the bathroom? Simple: they know that their man is turned on by sight. But after age thirty-five, the average male may be turned on more by kissing and caressing than by sight. So if you want to improve your sex life in the second half of marriage, pay more attention to what you do and less attention to what you see.

3. Balance the seesaw. We've found that from time to time we both need to lead in initiating sex. Not only do we reinforce our interest in sex but it helps stomp out boredom. Hormonal changes at this time of life actually bring couples into closer balance. "The male's shifting level of estrogen and testosterone may make him more willing to follow than to lead, happy for his wife to set the pace. And as a woman's estrogen declines and her testosterone becomes proportionately greater, she may become more assertive," say Kiester and Kiester.[7] Both changes can lead to a more compatible love life.

4. Dare to experiment. Because our response time may be longer, this is a great time in life to experiment. Remember, getting there can be half the fun. After thirty-three-plus years of marriage, we know we are less inhibited. Over the years, we have become more trusting of each other and more experienced. If you need to reestablish trust, you may want to use this chapter as a discussion starter. (Or see our Marriage Builder on page 102, entitled "Can We Talk about It?")

5. Achieve more from less. Frequency of intercourse in marriage is often emphasized; we know the statistics: the longer you are married, the less frequently you have sex. But little is written about the quality of the sexual experience. Our advice? Find whatever frequency works best for you. Let your times of lovemaking be anticipated and savored. Put less emphasis on how often and more emphasis on how good it is. We like what one husband said about sex and aging: "What I discovered was, as I got older, sex for its own sake wasn't much fun. But sex as a way of expressing love—that is sublime."

More good news:

> Studies show that older men who do strength training (lifting weights or working out against resistance on machines) as well as aerobics can rebuild their muscle power, make it much easier to lose unwanted pounds and inches, and actually improve physical and sexual prowess in defiance of biological clocks.[8]

Would not the same hold true for women? From our own experience, we've learned that when our backs are healthy and we are getting needed exercise, we have more enthusiasm and vigor for sex.

So now that we better understand how our bodies change as we age, how can we work with our bodies to enhance our love life? How can we rekindle romance?

STOKING YOUR MARITAL FIRES

When the kids leave home, it's time to rekindle romance. A friend told us, "By the time Hank and I made it to the empty nest, we had forgotten what romance was all about. For years we looked forward to the extra freedom and flexibility we would have in our love life when our last child left home, but now that it's happened, we're not sure we still have a love life! Can you help us?"

Do you identify with our friend? We offer our help, but only with the disclaimer that we're still trying to get it together ourselves. We don't think you ever arrive at a point where suddenly your love life is perfect.

We've already told you several times about how, over the years, we had developed the habit of overworking. So some of the time vacated by the departure of our sons was swallowed by more book deadlines, marriage seminars, and parenting groups.

Life for the Arps continued to accelerate until one day we realized we were working through weekends for the benefit of people working more sane hours. (This was soon after our disastrous experience in Toronto.) We were neglecting our marriage to help other couples build theirs! The pace of living in our empty nest had quickened until we finally looked at each other and said, "This is enough! Something has got to change!"

That's when we went to Europe for a few months. At the very beginning of our time there, we marked out a whole week and outlawed anything that resembled work!

The first couple of days we slept. Then we took long walks together. No phone calls, no beeping of the fax, no television blaring—just the Arps and the Alps. It's amazing what happens when you slow down, get away from the cares of the world, and focus on each other.

We realized that there would always be urgent needs or projects or books to write. If we didn't make choices, others would make them for us. That week, we evaluated where we were in our marriage and made hard choices and real commitments to simplify our lives and focus on each other and our mission.

We also read books and talked about how to spice up our love life. Old habits die hard. If you are a driven workaholic, like us, your love life may suffer. If you've spent the last twenty-five years focusing on your children, it takes work to refocus on your mate. A husband married for twenty-six years responded to our survey with this comment: "The greatest stress in our relationship is sex. My sex drive is overshadowed by my excessive compulsion to succeed in my career. When I get home, I'm just too tired."

At least he was beginning to see the reality of his situation. If you feel like two strangers, it will take effort to get reacquainted. But be encouraged—it can happen if you are willing to work at it.

Since our three months in Europe, things are slowly changing at the Arps'. The emphasis is on the word "slowly." Real change is hard work. It isn't simple to simplify our lives, but we are making progress. We've cut back on our writing schedule. We're planning more times away, times when we leave our work at home. And along the way, we are learning how to put fun and romance back into our relationship.

SIX SECRETS OF REKINDLING ROMANCE

Working on your love life has no age barrier. During one of our Marriage Alive seminars, Elizabeth, who had been married for forty years, told us about the struggles in the sexual relationship she shared with her husband: "We were older when we got married. I was twenty-nine and Alfred was thirty-two. We weren't so good in our love life. We tried a number of things that didn't work. I remember reading a book that was supposed to tell us what we needed, and I just wasn't like that. If Alfred had followed that book, he would have been all wrong!

"We were committed to each other, and at one point we gave up watching TV. It was taking up all our free time. As we began to explore different possibilities, I discovered I really liked to cuddle. Then we got a nice stereo system, and that helped put us in the mood and blocked outside noises. Sometimes it's the simple little things that actually made a difference in our love life."

As we work on "romancing" our own marriage and talk to other couples who are in the second half of marriage, like Elizabeth and Alfred, we've discovered several key ingredients for rekindling romance in long-term marriages. Hopefully, they will help you stoke your marital fires.

Be Affectionate

During a "Sweetheart's Banquet" at which we were speaking, an elderly couple came up after our talk, and sheepishly the wife told us, "When we were first married, someone suggested we shower together. We tried it and it was so much fun, we've been showering together every morning since!"

"Now that we aren't so agile," her husband added, "we can steady each other and prevent falls. Plus, after all the years it's still fun to wash each other's hair and backs. The shower is a great place to be affectionate!"

Romance isn't reserved just for the young, and neither is it reserved for the bedroom. Being affectionate, thoughtful, and kind at other times will spill over into your love life. We all like to be nurtured and cherished. Phone calls, notes that say, "I love you," cooking your mate's favorite dish, giving a bouquet of flowers, holding hands, a peck on the cheek, a wink across the room, and saying loving and endearing things to each other will add romance to your relationship.

Be a Listener

Two of the most important lovemaking skills and romance enhancers are listening with your heart and talking to your spouse while you are loving each other. Your love life may be active, but if it is all action and no talk, you're missing an added dimension of romance. Tell your mate what you like. Use a little body language. Nobody is a mind reader!

If you find it difficult to talk about the intimate side of your relationship, start by reading a book together. You may find that this is less threatening, and it may open the door for conversation—and who knows what doors conversation may open! Or use the Marriage Builder at the end of the chapter.

Be Adventuresome

Add some adventure. Try a little spontaneity. If you always make love in the evening, try mornings. Call in late for work and grab a couple of hours with each other while you are fresh. Plan a middle-of-the-day rendezvous. One couple, who both work downtown, took a picnic basket to work and met at a downtown motel on their lunch break. Another couple, on a more austere budget, met during their afternoon break in their car in the parking garage for hugs and kisses. Go on and brainstorm. You're only limited by your imagination! Try some variety in when and where you make love. Remember, variety can be the spice of life. Be explorers.

Be Playful

Our friends Dave and Jeanne love rabbits and have four (the stuffed variety) that always travel with them. When we visited them recently, we personally met their rabbits and discovered rabbit decorating themes all over their house! The rabbits were usually in pairs—just like Dave and Jeanne, who in retirement are usually together. They may be older, but their playful spirit and love of romance has blossomed with years. Romance depends on your attitude and perspective. For instance, Jeanne laughingly said, "What might be considered sexual harassment at work can bring enjoyment and pleasure at home!"

The empty nest is a great time to enter our second childhood. Too often we take ourselves and our mates too seriously. Or we always hurry. Remember, whatever you do to promote romance, getting there is half the fun. Making time for love will help you be good to each other. Take time to unwind from your busy day; make the transition slowly. Go for a walk and hold hands. Stop along the way for a kiss or two. Taking time to kiss and cuddle and laugh and share intimate thoughts during your lovemaking will add romance.

Be in Shape

In our forties, we realized we weren't as agile as we thought. Stress, teenagers, and yard work had taken their toll. This was about the time

Claudia injured her back, requiring several months of therapy. Part of her therapy program was to work out with light weights and do numerous exercises. Not only did this benefit her back, it helped her general physical condition so much that Dave decided (under duress) to join her.

Having lived on overload for so long, it seemed strange to take time to work out together. But it has had great benefits—even in the bedroom!

Sometimes romance in the empty nest is zapped by the battle of the bulge. As we age, it's natural—regardless of what the TV ads say—to put on a little padding. Thin may be "in" in our culture, but for the older population, being too thin can be a health hazard. Whatever our scales register, we can improve our fitness and firmness by regular exercise. Fitness walking several times each week gives us energy and helps us stay in shape. Face it, when you feel good about your body, you feel better about romance! So we encourage you to keep physically fit. Walk and exercise for your love life. You won't regret it!

Note: Not everything is cured by walking and exercise. If you have a medical problem or take medication that interferes with your love life, talk with your physician. There may be a simple solution, and it's certainly to your benefit to check it out! A yearly physical is a good investment in the health of your marriage.

Be a Little Wacky

What can you do to jolt your own established patterns? What can you do that is a little out of character? A fun getaway at Shakertown in Kentucky was a little out of character for us. To appreciate this romantic interlude, you need to know your history. Shakertown is basically a museum because the population has totally died out. You see, they practiced celibacy. Each house had separate doors for the women and for the men. Everything was separate. Just walking through the old houses and buildings in the town gave us a real feeling of history. As we stood for some time in the little graveyard, we wondered what kinds of lives those people experienced. Did they have romantic feelings for each other? Did they fall in love? Did they slip away and break the celibacy rules?

Later that evening, as we broke the rules, we thought, *What a great location for empty-nest couples who want to do something creative that is just a little off the wall.* If you live near Kentucky, we recommend Shaker-town, but wherever you live, we recommend a weekend getaway. Nothing helps revive romance like focused time away together.

If your budget is limited, be creative. Our friends Joseph and Linda love camping getaways. Other couples trade houses and condos. Maybe you have adult children who would loan you their homes when they are away. When our oldest son and daughter-in-law lived in Williamsburg, Virginia, they offered us their apartment when they were going to be away for several weeks. Imagine our surprise when we arrived to find the table romantically set for two, with candles and their best china! Go on and think creatively. Plan a getaway for yourselves! (See Marriage Builder on page 132 for tips on how to design a weekend getaway.)

LEARN TO PACE YOURSELF

We look forward to growing old together and loving each other along the way, but we are learning that if that is going to happen, we must pace ourselves. We try to control our schedule instead of having it control us, as in our Toronto experience. But there are still times we must fly a lot or make multiple trips. Recently we knew it was time to regroup when we got on the hotel elevator and punched the number for the floor our room was on in the previous city! But even though we still get in hectic situations, we are handling them with a little more savvy. For example, on a recent business trip to Grand Rapids, Michigan, we set our alarm and got up early, and before our long, hectic day of meetings, we took time for us. Making personal time for ourselves before we started made the whole day go better.

The next city, we continued to invest time in us. That Saturday morning in Minneapolis, we took a long walk. We mean a really long walk! As we walked, we talked and forgot how far we were walking. Exhausted but relaxed, we got back to our room about noon to get ready for our afternoon meeting. We had left the "Do not disturb" sign on our door all morning, because we wanted to shower and freshen up before the maid cleaned our room.

At about 1:00 P.M. we left our room and took the sign off our door. As we were walking down the hall, Dave was still talking about how far we had walked when he said, "Claudia, you wore me out! We overdid it! You did me in!"

"Well," Claudia responded, "I feel great! I feel invigorated!"

We ran into the maid, so Dave told her, "We're out of room 401 for a little while. You can clean it now."

The maid's funny look clued us in that she had heard our entire conversation. Guess she wondered what this older couple had been doing in their room all morning! We laughed all the way to our car.

As we reflected on our trip to Toronto and then on our trip to Grand Rapids and Minneapolis, we thought: two stressful trips but two completely different experiences. What made the difference? We had learned to pace ourselves, to make personal time a priority, and to find time for loving each other.

We hope you will find time to pace yourself, to stoke your own fire, and make your love relationship a priority. Take it from our friends Dave and Jeanne: it can just keep getting better and better as the years go by. "Romance doesn't have to die out," said Dave. "It can grow and blossom through all your married years, if you continue to show your love in physical ways plus loving words and deeds. God designed man and woman to enjoy each other in marriage, and we find that enjoyment still growing after forty-five years of marriage."

Let us encourage you to fan the fires of romance in your empty nest. You never know where it might lead. Go on and take the risk. Stoke your own fire and enjoy the second half of marriage with your lover and your best friend!

❧

MARRIAGE BUILDER

Conversation Opener — "Let's Talk about Sex"

1. When you got married, how well prepared were you for the sexual relationship?

2. Did you have any difficulties in the early adjustment period? How well did you deal with these?

3. Were your sexual needs different (for example, in frequency or intensity)?

4. How have you adjusted to your different needs over the years?

5. Has there been a change in your sexual relationship since you moved into the second half of marriage? If so, have you both been able to accept this and adjust to it?

6. What changes would you like to make at the present time?[9]

Challenge Seven

✤

*Adjust to Changing Roles with Aging Parents
and Adult Children*

For me, the emotional drain of trying to be everything to everybody is affecting my relationship with my husband. There is no energy left at the end of the day for me or to invest in our marriage.

—wife married for twenty-eight years

I look forward to that time in life of being somewhat free of feeling responsible for other people's problems.

—wife married for forty-seven years

I'm frightened that we are draining our own resources for our latter years, caring for my parents. It makes me feel very insecure.

—husband married for thirty-two years

We don't have an empty nest yet, although two out of three are gone. We've tried to push our children out of the nest but leave the lines of communication open to advise and assist when needed.

—husband married for thirty years

Whatever I do for my parents, I can never meet all of their expectations. Yet I keep trying. I'd have to say unmet expectations are the hardest to deal with. I need to add that my expectations for a close relationship with them generally go unmet, and that is a big disappointment to me.

—wife married for thirty-one years

Life is an opportunity for every person to create a new story that can be passed along by generations to come.

—anonymous

The greatest stress in my marriage," one wife in our survey responded, "is being caught between a teenage son who makes such foolish choices and my elderly dad, who needs to be cared for. Time and energy to invest in my twenty-year marriage is nonexistent."

Others in our survey confirmed that intergenerational stress is a major issue in the second half of marriage. How can you build your marriage in the middle of the family seesaw—adolescent or adult children and maybe even grandchildren on one end, and aging parents on the other end? You love your family on both ends, but you also love your spouse, who should be your first priority. How can you find balance? One mother asked, "I've been married for twenty-three years. I have two sons, ages fourteen and nineteen, and I'm kind of looking forward to the empty nest; is that terribly abnormal?"

"No," we told her, "not at all!"

HOW EMPTY IS YOUR NEST?

The term "empty nest" paints an unrealistic picture. Your home may be emptied of children, but your love and concern for them never empties. Or sometimes the nest refills, when children return and perhaps bring spouses and/or grandchildren to live with you. Or the nest may never really empty. Of unmarried American men between the ages of twenty-five and thirty-four, more than one third are still living at home.[1]

One wife, who has been married for forty-eight years, responded to our survey by saying, "Really, we never had an empty nest. My widowed mother lived with us—in her own apartment in our home—for twenty-five years. One son left home, lived on his own for a while, and then returned to live with us. My mother died about a year ago at ninety-two, and my son, his wife, and their baby moved into my mom's apartment. Consequently, we've never experienced an empty nest. For years we've been members of the 'sandwich generation.'"

Our children have never returned home to live with us, but we'll always remember the first time they all came home to visit during the Christmas after Jonathan left for college. Everyone was spread out around the country, and we were looking forward to all being together again. But we weren't so delighted when we found out they all wanted to bring their cats—a total of five! Let it never be said the Arps are not good hosts. We went right out and bought a cat condo so that all the cats would have a fun place to play and sleep—and perhaps ignore our furniture. We have never been a major indoor pet family. We did have our share of hamsters, guinea pigs, and goldfish, but living for years in an apartment in Vienna, Austria, didn't encourage big-time pet ownership.

By the time we moved back to the States, our children were older, and we realized that any cats or dogs we might adopt would outlive our kids' childhood years. So when our boys claimed they would be emotionally damaged for life if we didn't get a cat or dog, we told them, "When you grow up, you can have all the pets you want." The rest is history—and they were all coming to visit!

We have to admit, that was a unique family reunion. Five cats offered free entertainment. Was it fun? At times we would say, "Yes." It was one visit when frustrations centered around cats and not family members and personalities. No one complained of being bored. There were no overheated discussions. Instead, there was always a cat or two around to laugh at.

Even today we chuckle when we think of our Arp cat convention. Over the years, humor and flexibility have helped us balance a marriage perched in the middle of our family's generational seesaw. Two things we have learned: first, look for humor; second, grab love where you find it! Let's look closer at some common relationship issues with aging parents and adult children. How can you make your marriage a priority while balancing the generational seesaw?

RELATING TO ELDERLY PARENTS

Family pressure is like an old friend who is hard to get along with—it can be a love-hate relationship. Everyone wants to be needed, but there is a thin line between need and manipulation. Our friend George related his story:

"Growing up, I never had a close relationship with my mother, but when my dad passed away, I wanted to be there for Mom and take care of her needs. We lived in a neighboring town, so I could check on her often. The first couple of years went great. She was appreciative of all the things my wife, Ida, and I did for her. I handled her finances and listened to her stories time and time again. Then our four daughters began to marry and start their own families. Just as our family relationships were expanding—and we were needed more on the other side of the generational seesaw—Mom became more demanding. Now she gets upset when we announce the upcoming arrival of another grandchild. Her comment 'There will just be more and more' gives an indication of her nonverbal message: 'And for me, I'll get less and less of your time and attention.'

"How can we let Mom know we love her and will take care of her but that we can't meet her needs for companionship—and we're sick and tired of hearing of her aches and pains, while she cares little for our own? When we have any medical problems at all, she just ignores us. Recently Ida had unscheduled minor surgery on the day I was supposed to visit Mom. She was more upset about the delay in my visit than interested in how Ida was getting along. Comments like 'Well, come see me when you can and when you want to' make me want to get in the car and go the opposite direction! I love my mom, but her manipulative demands are driving me crazy. When she continually asks, 'Honey, when are you coming?' I want to scream, 'Never!'"

"She had always been pleasant to Ida, but she seems less satisfied when we visit her together. To put it bluntly, it's me she wants around, and she wants me by herself. For years she talked about just the two of us taking a trip together. At times she even bought new clothes to wear on 'our trip.' Finally I decided it was easier to take her somewhere than to listen to her. We went to the beach for four days; then Ida and our youngest daughter joined us. Our four days together went quite well, but Mom blew it when later she told me, 'It's too bad the others had to come. It was better when it was just the two of us.' Mom doesn't realize that in my life when it is 'just the two of us,' that is supposed to be me and Ida—not me and Mom!"

Do you identify with George? Can you imagine how Ida feels? How can they build their marriage in the midst of family pressure from George's mom?

Other seesaw scenarios include elderly parents living with a couple—some pleasant situations and some not. Our friend Mary told us about the year and a half that her mother-in-law lived with her and Glenn. They still had two adolescents at home, and Glenn's mother was all too quick to tell her grandchildren what to do.

"The hardest part," Mary told us, "was when she would contradict what we had already told our teenagers. It was confusing for them. Her failing health was the reason she moved in with us. Glenn was her only child, but the daily care for her was on my shoulders. At that time Glenn was traveling quite a bit. Often he would ask me to go on a business trip with him, and I would reply, 'I'd love to, honey, but someone needs to be here for your mother.'

"This got very old! So one time when he asked me to go away with him, I answered, 'Yes, yes, I can!' We hired someone to come into our home and stay with her. One mistake I made was not doing that sooner. Someone needs to take care of the caretaker. After a year and a half, we moved and were able to move Glenn's mother into her own little house right next to ours. We hired someone to come in daily to be with her. That worked much better, and there was less tension in my relationship with Glenn."

Have you ever noticed that as people age, they tend to grow more saintly, loving, and caring, or they become more bitter, complaining, and self-centered? While you can't choose for your parents how they will be in old age, you can choose for yourself! History does not have to repeat itself.

It may help us, in relating to our family seesaw, to understand that each generation, from adolescence to the elderly, wants the same things. We all have the same basic physiological needs for food and shelter. But we also need to love and be loved. We need affection and tenderness, respect and dignity, acceptance, honesty, trust, and hope. And as much as is possible, we need freedom from pain. Which of these needs can we, as adult children, provide for our parents? Much of your answer may depend on your present relationship with your parents.

IDENTIFY POTENTIAL PROBLEMS

Whatever the situation, your relationship with your elderly parents affects your marriage. Whether the effect is positive or negative depends more on you than on the situation. A negative situation can bring you closer together as a couple as you seek to find a solution you can all live with. Let's begin by looking at typical problems in relating to elderly parents.

Lack of trust. If parents have little trust and respect for their adult children, it will be hard for them to have a close relationship. In such a situation, a better relationship may require that the son or daughter be more independent and that the relationship with the parent be more distant. Not all elderly parent–adult-child relationships are close. If your relationship with your parents is healthy and close, be thankful! It is one of life's blessings. If it isn't close, do what you can do, but realize that some things may never change.

Lack of adult status. Sometimes the parent fails to treat the son or daughter as an adult. "Within two minutes, she has reduced me to a ten-year-old," complained our friend Millie. "I get so frustrated. I'm over fifty and have married children myself, but when I'm around Mom, I instantly become the child. Recently, in a conversation with Mom, she said, 'Millie, I just don't know what will ever happen to your brother.' I responded, 'Mom, he's fifty-eight years old. He's already happened!'

"I can't control Mom or keep her from worrying and treating my brother and me as children, but I can change me and how I relate to my own adult children. I don't want to be an eighty-three-year-old mother standing at the sink, saying, 'I don't know what will ever happen to my sixty-year-old son!'"

Denial. If there is little honest communication in your relationship with your parents, it will be harder to help them in their old age. One survey participant told us how his dad would not discuss the future: "He lives daily in denial. It's been months since he was physically able to drive a car, but he still talks all the time about getting a new van. There is no way I can get him to consider moving into a retirement community—yet since my mom died, his health has failed, and he just won't be able to manage living alone for much longer. Plus, he is getting more forgetful in handling his finances and other affairs, but he won't let me help him. I'm an only child. What can I do?"

Excessive demands and manipulation. Along with the demanding parent is the one who is manipulative. "My mom is like an emotional octopus," another survey participant wrote. "She attaches her emotional tentacles to me and sucks out my patience and energy. Her favorite line is, 'I just called to let you know I'm getting along all right, so you won't worry.' The real message is, 'If you cared, you would have called first to see how I am.'"

LEAVE AND HONOR

Some biblical truths must be held in tension with each other. On the one hand, we are told to leave our parents; on the other hand, to honor them. Genesis 2:24 instructs us to leave our mother and father and to cleave to our mate. We need to switch our family allegiance. A marriage in which one mate refuses to realign his priority from his parents to his spouse—or in which one or both of the parents expect their son or daughter to put them before their mate—will have problems. Cleaving to parents isn't biblical and doesn't work.

However, this Scripture is not an excuse to withhold care for parents as they age. In the Ten Commandments, we are told to honor our mothers and fathers, and this has no expiration date or conditions. It doesn't say honor your parents until you are twenty-one, nor does it say honor your parents if they deserve it and treat you with respect. In the Scriptures, it is clear that for us as children (even sixty-year-old children), our part of the deal is not dependent on how loving, caring, and understanding our parents are.

THE MARRIAGE BALANCING ACT

At this point we need to refocus. You may want to use the Marriage Builder "Our Needs, Their Needs," at the end of the chapter, to get some perspective on your individual situation. Although we offer a few suggestions, this chapter is not about relating to parents. This is a book about building your marriage for the second half, and you need to continue to invest in your marriage while loving, honoring, and caring for your aging parents. So let's look at what we can do.

Look for the Positive

A saying we repeat often is, "We can do what we can do, and that's what we can do." This may need to become your motto, too, if you want to successfully meet this challenge in the second half of your marriage. Maybe you are blessed with parents who are positive, are in excellent health, and each day look for the best.

Or you may be in a more distressing situation. You may have to look harder to find the positive, but we challenge you to look until you find something. One husband in our survey, who had been married for thirty-four years, wrote that it is all relative: "The empty nest is stressful, but inherently it is not as stressful as raising children." To build positive bridges, consider the following possibilities:

Collect family history. When you are with your parents, sidetrack the "body recital" by asking questions about when they were younger. You may want to take notes or tape record this for family history. Note taking is a good way to occupy your mind, especially when the story being told is a repeat. We talk at around one hundred words a minute (older people tend to talk much slower), but we can think at around four hundred words per minute.[2] Because we think faster than we speak, it is harder to listen to the other person, especially if we have already heard about the gall bladder operation numerous times.

Recently one of our sons, in a phone conversation, encouraged his granddad to talk about his experience in World War II. While they talked, he took notes on his computer and then E-mailed the family a little bit of our family history. We remember Dave's grandmother telling us about her first car—the first car in her county—and how she forged streams to get to the next town. We have the blanket she used in that car to cover up her legs to keep warm. Talk about a piece of family history!

Collect family wisdom. Write down sayings that would be interesting to others in the family. Sayings like "I was just born too soon" or "You're as cute as an Indian rubber bouncing ball" help us appreciate the unique characters that our parents are!

Make a positive list. Turn back to the Marriage Builder on page 160 and look at the list of positive feelings words. List things that are positive about your mom and/or dad. Remember, we often forget to express the tender feelings and thoughts we have about our loved ones. As you did with your spouse, write out several positive sentences and then use them the next time you talk to your parent.

Do something out of character. Dave's family was never a "Let's eat out" family, and as his parents aged, they ate out less and less. So when we suggested taking his dad out for a steak dinner to celebrate his eighty-fourth birthday, we were surprised when he enthusiastically agreed. We chose a restaurant he had never been to before even though he has lived in the same city for over thirty years. It was out of character but was a delightful evening for all. Now when we want to give him a special gift, we can give him a gift certificate to that restaurant!

Do something they want to do. Give your elderly parent a gift of love. For Claudia's mother, that could be a shopping trip to Atlanta. But plan ahead. While parents usually like surprises, half of the fun may be the anticipation. Knowing you are coming to visit or are going to call may be as enjoyable as the actual event.

Provide lots of pictures. From time to time we will put together little photo albums and send them to our parents. It helps them keep up with grandchildren and great-grandchildren. You may want to do the same. Write the names, the date, and the occasion on the back of each picture. Include the middle name if it happens to be the name of one of your parents. They may have forgotten that a great-grandchild was named after them!

Realize That Life Goes On

You may have heard about the elderly couple who after sixty-five years of marriage went to the lawyer to get a divorce. "Why, after all these years together," the bewildered lawyer asked them, "do you want to get a divorce?"

"Oh," answered the husband, "we were waiting for our children to die."

While no one we know would say they are "waiting for their parents to die," it is possible to put our head in the sand like the ostrich and not face the present and future with objectivity. Whatever your situation with your aging parents, you need to build your own marriage now—not in the future when you have less stress. So take the following four tips:

Deal with false guilt. You simply can't be all things to all people. Remember, you can do what you can do, and that's what you can do.

Don't feel responsible for what you can't control. Anxiety tends to appear when we feel responsible for things we can't control. So remember the prayer used in Alcoholics Anonymous: "God, grant me the serenity to accept the things I cannot change, courage to change the things I can, and wisdom to know the difference." You may even want to make a list of what you can do and can't do.

Get advice from others. Older friends have been a great source of information for us. Observe those with healthy extended family relationships. Ask questions. Read books. Do whatever you can to gather helpful information.

Get a life. Whatever your situation with your aging parents, you need a life of your own. And your marriage needs maintenance, especially in these stressful years.

RELATING TO OUR ADULT CHILDREN

On the other side of the generational seesaw, we face similar issues, but we are the parents! The transition into adult relationships with our children and their spouses can be a difficult challenge and if not well managed can greatly affect our own marriage. Earlier we said that each generation has the same basic needs. Let's look at life from the perspective of the young adult. Then we will consider potential problems and possible solutions.

A VIEW FROM THE OTHER SIDE

One young wife who responded to our survey gave some insight into this stage of life, from a young adult's perspective: "I'm twenty-six years old, and the complaint that I and most of my friends have is that our parents become so needy and insecure during this 'empty nest' stage. Their hugs and kisses become very aggressive, and they begin to cross a lot of relational boundaries. I know they want my love, but this behavior just drives me away. I want to be around a parent who is confident and self-assured and one who respects my boundaries. All of that intense bear-hugging, cheek-pinching business really drives kids away. At least, it does for me and all of my friends. I feel that boundaries really do allow for more freedom in relationships. I just thought I would say this, because it's something many of us don't feel comfortable telling our parents when they go through this stage. It has a bearing on their relationship with their kids, which feeds their self-esteem in a way that affects a huge part of their lives."

IDENTIFY POTENTIAL PROBLEMS AND SOLUTIONS

From this young woman's comments, we can immediately identify several potential areas of stress in parent–adult-children relationships. Many are the same issues we face with our own parents—lack of trust, lack of adult status, and interfering instead of respecting boundaries. The difference being, we are on the other side of life.

The issue of boundaries is closely related to lack of adult status and lack of trust. Are we willing to let go—to release our children into adulthood and let them lead their own lives? If we hope to have healthy relationships with our adult children, it is critical that we respect their boundaries.

Needy and insecure parents may be basing their sense of self-worth on their children—or leaning too much on their children and not on their mate. This is an unfair burden for any child and especially for an adult child, who has enough struggles coping with the new responsibilities of adulthood. When survey participants indicated that the best aspect of their marriage was their children and their grandchildren, it usually followed that their marital satisfaction was at a very low level.

Healthy relationships with your adult children will enrich your second-half marriage. While it may be difficult to build a more adult relationship with your children, it is possible. Many of those who responded to our survey offered suggestions for surmounting this challenge. Following are some of their comments.

A wife who had been married for thirty years wrote, "When our first daughter left home to go to college, I felt as if she had died. I knew she hadn't, but I suddenly realized that our family unit as we had known it and had constructed it for twenty years was over. I went through a grieving process of about six months. I believe our whole family grieved for the death of our family unity. It was a process. Now ten years later we know that the leaving gave new birth to an entire new dimension in family relationships. Spouses from different cultures have been added to give richness and diversity. Grandchildren have brought the joy of discovery and the fascination of fantasy back into our home. God is so faithful. All we can do is praise him."

A husband wrote, "From the time your kids are twelve or thirteen—actually, from birth—you need to have an active plan and vision for letting them go. This involves equipping them for the decisions they will need to make in the future. You also need to let them make more of their own decisions, even at the risk of them making mistakes. I think that with our oldest child, we held on too tight, causing a lack of self-confidence."

A mother, married for thirty-three years, gave this tip: "Do something to bring closure. I made 'going away to school' afghans for each of my sons. It took several years for each one. When each boy left for college, he got his afghan. For me it was like being able to tie up loose ends. When the afghan was finished, I was somehow able to let go."

A dad, married for thirty-two years, encouraged us to be available if needed. "All three of our children," he wrote, "at one time or other came back to live with us for some months. As they got out in the world, they learned that their parents and home were a refuge. They had taken us for granted, not really knowing what was out there."

WHAT ABOUT MARRIED CHILDREN?

When our children marry, the family circle expands and relationships become more complicated. All of these relationships affect our marriage. So here are the "best of the best" tips we received for keeping in-law relationships positive:

> *"Build the relationship with each couple. Some of your best times will be couple to couple."*
>
> *"Visit each couple, but not too often or don't stay too long."*
>
> *"Let them parent their own children."*
>
> *"Resist the urge to give advice."*
>
> *"Realize that you and your married children are not in the same season of life. You have very different goals."*
>
> *"Tolerate small irritations."*
>
> *"Build a relationship with each of your grandchildren."*
>
> *"Be interested in your children's professions, hobbies, and activities."*
>
> *"When you visit, find ways to participate in their household. Find the balance between pitching in and helping and being the guest."*

Now might be a good time to stop and evaluate your relationship with your adult children. You can use the Marriage Builder at the end of this chapter, entitled "Evaluating Your Relationship with Your Adult Children."

COMPLICATED FAMILY SITUATIONS—YOU DON'T KNOW OURS!

We've looked briefly at relationships with aging parents and with adult children. Either generation alone may challenge your marriage. How can you balance both at the same time? It's not always an easy assignment when there are conflicting needs on both sides just waiting to be met. And what about those family situations that are much more serious and complicated? With the high divorce rate and blended families, family relationships can get really complicated. Consider this recent letter to "Dear Abby":

Dear Abby,

I am the mother of a four-and-a-half-year-old. I have a problem getting into the Christmas spirit, and here's why: I worry about how to please everyone, since many people want to spend time with my daughter during the holidays.

My parents live next door. They want my daughter to wake up in their home on Christmas morning. Her biological father and his wife want time with her, and my husband's parents, who are divorced, each want to spend time with their granddaughter. Her father's parents also want to see her and shower her with gifts.

All of these people love my daughter very much and are involved in her life, but she's only one little girl, and I can't split her into six pieces. Please don't suggest that I invite them all to my home. It would never work. What should I do?

Perplexed

Dear Perplexed,

Make five slips of paper with the days of the week preceding Christmas (reserving the sixth day—Christmas Day—for you and your husband). Ask each relative to draw a day from the hat, and that will be *their* day to celebrate with your daughter. Good luck.[3]

Maybe you feel you need many slips of paper—and one that says, "I resign!" At this point, we need a slip of paper that says, "We don't know what to tell you to do!" We realize we haven't even touched the surface of how to deal with difficult family situations on either side of the generational seesaw. We haven't dealt with the adult child who totally rejects your values or chooses a lifestyle that makes you uncomfortable. We haven't given you five easy steps for living with adult children who temporarily or permanently move back home. We haven't addressed the pain of seeing a child go through an ugly divorce. What about hurting parents who are estranged from their adult children—who don't even talk with them or have contact with them? Or the precious grandchild who is being raised alone by a mom or dad who happens to be your son or daughter? How do you relate to your son and his live-in girlfriend?

Your marriage is greatly influenced by other family relationships. But when all is said and done, your marriage is the anchor relationship. That is the one relationship you can influence. Remember our motto: "You can do what you can do, and that's what you can do." And we have learned what to do with what we can't change.

In 1 Peter 5:7 are the comforting words, "Cast all your anxiety on him because he cares for you." When we cast our cares on our heavenly Father, we can say with the psalmist, "When I am afraid, I will trust in you. In God, whose word I praise, in God I trust; I will not be afraid" (Psalm 56:3–4). The validity of our faith in God shines through in situations that seem to have no earthly solutions. There is a release that comes when we give our cares to a God who loves us, and our family members, with a perfect love. If we put our life and our eternal future in God's hands, we can also trust him with our loved ones. And there is much comfort in this eternal truth!

YOU CAN BE A GENERATIONAL BRIDGE

In the end, we have to face the fact that some families are just closer than others. Some of us grew up in happy, healthy families, and others grew up in unhealthy families. Some of us started our marriages with liabilities but, over the course of our own marriage and family history, have turned them into assets to pass on to the next generation. It is possible to be a bridge between an unhealthy generation and a healthy generation. Listen to one survey participant, who is making that transition in her marriage and family:

"When my husband and I got married, my parents looked to us to fill all their social needs. We desired to meet new people our age and build relationships with them, as well as to spend time with my parents. My parents had no other friends to socialize with and therefore tried to plan our free time. As we learned how to set boundaries with my parents, we made a commitment to keep our friendships with others alive and healthy. In a few years we will have an empty nest, and we hope we will be available for our kids but not expect them to meet our social needs."

In closing, let us encourage you to be thankful for the healthy relationships that you have. Grab love where you find it! Accept what is realistic in your family, wherever you are in life. You can't go back and change your past family history, but what you do in the future is your choice. You can change the pattern. You can make a difference in future generations. You can pass down to your children and grandchildren a legacy of healthy family relationships and a marriage model worth following! And that's what you can do.

❧

MARRIAGE BUILDER

Our Needs, Their Needs

PERSON	NEEDS	HOW MET?		
		Me	Siblings	Other
Parent's present needs				
Our present needs				
Parent's future needs				
Our future needs				

Now think about the following questions. If possible, discuss them with your spouse.

1. What changes need to be made at the present time?

2. What changes will need to be made in the future?

3. What resources do we have to help make these changes (family, friends, other people, agencies, financial, and so forth)?

4. What can we do now to prepare for our future?

✌

MARRIAGE BUILDER

Evaluating Your Relationship with Your Adult Children

1. Is the amount of contact you have with your adult children
    a. too little?_____ b. too much?_____ c. about right?_____

    If you would like your answer to be different, what—if anything—can you do about changing it?

2. Do you have a good relationship with your grown children and their spouses?
    If not, is there any way you can make things better?

3. Are you satisfied with the way your grown children relate to you?
    For instance, when you need it, do they offer their help, encouragement, and so on? Do they express appreciation for the ways you help them?

4. Do you do all you can to demonstrate your love, appreciation, and gratitude to your grown children?

5. Do you maintain clear and open communication?

6. If a child of yours has been involved in divorce, have you been able to face the situation with as much understanding and tolerance as possible? If not, what can you do now to strengthen your relationship with your child?[4]

Challenge Eight

❧

Evaluate Where You Are on Your Spiritual Pilgrimage, Grow Closer to Each Other and to God, and Together Serve Others

The best aspects of our marriage are companionship, our faith in God, and our love for each other. We try to add to the other's happiness by surprising each other with little gifts, a hug, a kiss, or giving a compliment—or just being thoughtful.

—husband married for thirty-two years

I know a Christian couple going through a divorce now. They have been married for twenty-three years. This is very frightening to me. I know that I will always have to work at my marriage and never, ever take it for granted that it will just last without any effort.

—wife married for twenty-two years

Our marriage just keeps getting better and better. Our times with each other, sex, and ministering together are the best aspects of our marriage.

—husband and wife married for thirty-five years

The Lord has blessed us beyond measure. We brought to this marriage a background of healthy marriages and personal commitment to the Lord. We do homebound and nursing home visitation for our church. It's a wonderful outreach for us!

—husband married for seven years, second marriage
(They married after their first, long-term, happy marriages ended. Both of their first spouses passed away.)

He has taken me to the banquet hall, and his banner over me is love.

—Song of Songs 2:4

We believe that good marriages and spirituality should go hand in hand. However, there was one alarming trend we observed in our survey: of the participants (12 percent) who indicated that the best aspect of their marriage was the spiritual aspect, a high percentage of their other responses indicated much dissatisfaction with their marriage relationship. We have previously mentioned this trend, but now let's take a closer look.

A wife married for twenty-two years wrote, "The best aspect of my marriage is our commitment to each other and to Christ," then checked "very dissatisfied" for all the survey categories that dealt with the marriage relationship—like communication, conflict resolution, romance, and intimacy. What kind of Christian marriage did this couple have?

A husband married for nineteen years responded, "The best aspect of my marriage is putting God first," but then wrote, "The greatest stress in my marriage is too much negative communication and no respect."

It appears that for some, faith and commitment to God is the main reason they are staying in an unhappy marriage. One husband, who was in a second marriage and who was very dissatisfied in almost every category, wrote, "I know God will use all things for good." Then he added, "The greatest tension in my marriage is contention and strife."

What's wrong with this picture? Shouldn't our spiritual commitment improve the quality of our marriage? Faith in God should make a radical difference in our relationship with our spouse; it should enhance our love for each other. Something is terribly wrong if commitment to God is the only thing holding a marriage together. Marriage becomes a prison for dissatisfied mates instead of an oasis of love and acceptance and a place of refreshment and restoration.

In his book *Spheres of Love*, Stephen G. Post, Ph.D., associate professor at Case Western Reserve University, suggests that the high esteem that marriage once enjoyed has been difficult to sustain because it lacks what he defines as "a sacred canopy"—an affirmation of the significant foundational beliefs concerning the holy state of marriage.

Post writes, "The full dignity of marriage must be newly articulated," meaning that we must restate, in a way others can understand, the seriousness and status of marriage. Marriage is a solemn state taken too lightly by the world. Marriage was part of God's original natural order. Marriage transcends cultures. Marriage is a serious commitment—intended to be a permanent tie—and is the foundation of the family unit. Dr. Post adds, "Marriage is an essentially mysterious union like the mystical one between Christ and the church, should be entered reverently with the exchange of vows, and is a place where God dwells."[1]

Henri Nouwen, in *Seeds of Hope*, expands on the concept of marriage being a dwelling place for God:

> Marriage is not a lifelong attraction of two individuals to each other but a call for two people to witness together to God's love.... The real mystery of marriage is not that husband and wife love each other so much that they can find God in each other's lives but that God loves them so much that they can discover each other more and more as living reminders of God's presence. They are brought together, indeed, as two prayerful hands extended toward God and forming in this way a home for God in this world.[2]

How can we restore sanctity and sacredness to marriage? Let's look at what makes a marriage Christian.

WHAT MAKES A MARRIAGE CHRISTIAN?

The word "marriage" can have many meanings. Even the term "Christian marriage" can be interpreted in a number of ways. The Bible records the stories of godly men who had polygamous marriages that would not be recognized today as meeting Christian standards. Also in biblical times, marriages were arranged and women did not have the same legal rights and status as men.

Today the basic requirements of a Christian marriage are monogamy (one man and one woman), fidelity (sex exclusively with the marriage partner), a lifelong commitment (although the Bible allows divorce under some circumstances, a Christian marriage should mean a lifelong commitment), and mutual consent (no longer are marriages arranged and forced).

It seems that over the years, the church has emphasized requirements and conditions that must be met for the wedding ceremony to take place but then had very little to say about how to maintain the sacredness of marriage or the quality of the relationship during all the years that follow. The church has failed to build a sacred canopy of protection over marriage and has also failed to teach the personal relationship skills needed to sustain it. No wonder Christian marriages are breaking up in record numbers! It is time to stop this trend. It is time to elevate marriage to a sacred state.

THE SACRED CANOPY OF MARRIAGE

Stephen Post's concept of a sacred canopy struck home with us. We think a sacred canopy is an essential component to a loving Christian marriage.

What do you think of when you think of the word "canopy"? Our preliminary word study revealed these concepts: a protective covering or shelter from life's storms, a haven, a refuge, a retreat, a sanctuary, a place of safety. Would not we all desire these words to describe our marriage?

What do you think of when you apply the word "sacred" to the state of marriage? We thought of the words "consecrated," "divine," "holy," "ordained," "sanctioned," "pure," "revered." Certainly all these words describe a truly Christian marriage.

Finally, we studied the word "marriage." And we found terms like "union," "match," "wedlock," "consortium," and "conjugality." If that's all that marriage is, it sure doesn't sound that great!

Then the light went on! It's God's sacred canopy that elevates marriage and makes it a holy institution. Dr. Post reiterates that it is Christianity that provides marriage with the theological roots that make marriage a lifetime commitment in a world that seems incapable of anything more than "limited engagements." "Marriage fails," he writes, "for many reasons, one of which is the lack of a foundation in meanings of any ultimate significance."[3]

Does your marriage have a sacred canopy? What are your basic beliefs about what elevates your marriage? Is your marriage a lifetime commitment? Are you committed to fidelity? Are you committed to marital growth? What are the distinctive marks that set your marriage apart as a Christian marriage? Is it the loving way you relate to one another? Do the words "creativity" and "service" describe aspects of your marriage?

So many times as we search for deeper spiritual truths dealing with marriage, we return to our mentors, David and Vera Mace. And from our own personal observations, the words "creativity" and "service" describe David and Vera Mace. When others their age were retiring and rocking on their porches, they continued—well into their eighties—to speak and train couples in marriage enrichment. And as a widow at ninety-two, Vera coauthored a paper with us for the United Nation's International Year of the Family. She is an amazing lady, and we will always be grateful for what she and David have meant to us.

In their book *What's Happening to Clergy Marriages?* the Maces share their core beliefs. These five beliefs, if adopted (and acted upon), could form the sacred canopy for your marriage!

1. We believe that it was God who brought us together in the first place.
2. We believe that our continuing life together is part of the divine purpose.

3. We believe that we have a witness to bear together.
4. We believe that our shared life must have a sacrificial quality.
5. We believe that our Christian marriage must find spiritual expression.[4]

We challenge you to build a sacred canopy over your marriage. Then you can have a marriage that is truly Christian. Our faith in God, and our beliefs about Christian marriage, should make a radical difference in our relationship with our spouse.

OPEN YOUR HEART

In *To Understand Each Other*, Dr. Tournier wrote,

> God is passionately interested in each human being. To receive God is also, therefore, to receive his intense interest for those with whom we have rubbed shoulders without really seeming to understand them. [This could be your mate!] It is impossible to open one's heart to God without also opening it to one's fellow.[5]

It is God who can open your eyes and heart and give you a new passion for your mate and help you build a sacred canopy for your marriage. He can give you a new passion to understand your spouse. "As soon as a person feels understood," Tournier continues, "he opens up, and because he lowers his defenses, he is also able to make himself better understood."[6]

RELATIONSHIP IS THE KEY!

To have a truly Christian marriage, couples must have an open, honest relationship with each other. Couples who are able to construct their own sacred marriage canopy, surmount this eighth midlife challenge (as well as the other seven), and build a companionship marriage can be to others a living example of an enriched Christian marriage.

A friend challenged us: "Wait a minute. I like the idea of the sacred marriage canopy and having a more egalitarian, companionship marriage. But doesn't the Bible teach more of a hierarchical style of marriage? A companionship marriage sounds like what I would like to experience, but is this style of marriage in harmony with the Scriptures?"

Our friend asked a very relevant question and one that deserves a thorough answer. Following is our perspective, which has more to do with the *quality* of the relationship than the *style* of marriage.

IS A COMPANIONSHIP MARRIAGE CHRISTIAN?

Before we look closer at the value of a companionship marriage, let's briefly define both styles of marriage. We are not saying that a companionship marriage is more or less "Christian" than a traditional, hierarchical marriage. Both have a basis in the Scriptures. Ephesians 5:21–33 models the hierarchical style of marriage. However, we must note that a hierarchical marriage as related by this passage of Scripture is not domineering or authoritarian. It simply puts the man as the head (as was the cultural pattern of that day). Dr. Mace states, "The hierarchical view of marriage is in no sense distinctively Christian. It has been universal among all the major human civilizations—including the Hebrew tradition."[7] The emphasis in this passage is on the husband's sacrificial love for his wife as Christ loved the church. Also, it begins with the verse "Submit to one another out of reverence for Christ" (Ephesians 5:21). In any marriage, power plays and manipulation will destroy the potential for love.

Genesis 2:24 pictures the companionship style. One of the purposes of marriage, given in Genesis 2:18, is to provide companionship in a close and nurturing relationship, because God saw that it was "not good for the man to be alone."

While Jesus had very little to say about marriage, he quoted Genesis 2:24 (when asked if it was lawful to divorce) and expounded on it:

"Haven't you read," he replied, "that at the beginning the Creator 'made them male and female,' and said, 'For this reason a man will leave his father and mother and be united to his wife, and the two will become one flesh'? So they are no longer two, but one. Therefore what God has joined together, let man not separate."

—Matthew 19:4–6

Throughout the New Testament, Jesus emphasized loving relationships. He talked about the supreme importance of loving our neighbor as we love ourselves. In the New Testament, the word "neighbor" means that person who is nearest and dearest to you. Stop and think about who your closest neighbor is. If you are married, it's your mate! So what Jesus taught and modeled about relationships has particular application to the marriage relationship.

Drs. David and Vera Mace add the historical background of the development of this style of marriage. They remind us that all marriages were structured hierarchically until the advent of democracy, which, by giving men and women the right to vote, introduced a revolution of gigantic proportions. The coming of the companionship marriage was a direct reflection of that democratic ideal.[8]

So where does this leave Christian marriages today? The Maces, in their book *Marriage Enrichment in the Church*, write,

> The Bible gives some support to both the hierarchical and the companionship concepts of marriage. Both of them fulfill such basic requirements as monogamy, fidelity, and the intention of lifelong commitment. Both have worked well for Christians at different periods of history [and we might add, at different stages of a marriage]. So instead of arguing about one being right and the other wrong, the best conclusion probably is that a Christian couple may take their choice; but they had better make quite sure, from the beginning, that they are both making the same choice!
>
> One final point must be made. No matter which marriage pattern you choose, you'll have to work at the relationship to bring it up to a truly Christian level.... So take your choice! But either way, the achievement of a mature Christian marriage will not be easy. It will be a lifelong task. But it will yield great rewards.[9]

YOUR SPIRITUAL PILGRIMAGE

Perhaps our objective should not be to identify a Christian marriage style but rather to be a better Christian within marriage. The quality of the relationship is the key issue in a Christian marriage, not the form or style. Wherever you are on your spiritual pilgrimage, how can you love and serve your spouse? And how can you love God and serve others?

The true expression of faith in God will result in practical application. We have three suggestions for continuing your spiritual journey. First, accept where both you and your spouse are on that journey at present. Second, promote spiritual closeness and unity through dialogue, devotions, and/or prayer together. Third, together serve others.

Accept Where You Both Are on Your Spiritual Journey

"The greatest stress in our marriage is that we are at different places spiritually," responded a survey participant, married for nineteen years. Most couples are at different places, but it doesn't have to be stressful—not if we're willing to accept diversity in the expression of our Christian faith.

We often hear comments like "But my mate isn't as spiritual as I am" or "We absolutely can't pray together." While most Christian couples would desire more spiritual intimacy, we can let our diversity enrich our relationship rather than divide us.

Most importantly, you must be on a spiritual journey, your journey must have your attention, and your journey must be a priority. Within that framework, we can have different expressions of our faith and service. One couple may have a rich devotional and prayer life together. Another couple may not be as comfortable praying together but enjoy and receive much meaning from helping to build houses for Habitat for Humanity. A third couple may be active in their church, but the husband finds using his musical talents in the choir as most meaningful, while his wife gains satisfaction and meaning from teaching the third graders in Sunday school.

For those who are at different places in your spiritual pilgrimage, we offer the following suggestions:

Don't force or coerce your spouse to attend or do something with you that you know he or she will not enjoy. God does not force us to do things against our will—so let him be your model.

Be teachable and willing to learn. Whatever road you take, be willing to learn from others. Someday you may look back with amusement, acknowledging that you were not as smart as you thought you were. With being teachable comes the need to grow and change, so watch out for close-mindedness and rigidity. Be open for God's Spirit to teach, lead, guide, and enlighten you.

Realize that one of the privileges and joys of a marriage is only having to relate one to one. You don't have to settle theological or denominational issues or settle disputes among countries or even factions in your church or group. A little diversity can spice up your relationship!

Promote Spiritual Closeness

Our relationship to God should foster marital closeness, and nothing brings us closer together than praying together. Tournier agrees. He says that praying together is the highest tie binding a couple together and yet it is rare:

> Happy are the couples who do recognize and understand that their happiness is a gift of God, who can kneel together to express their thanks not only for the love which he has put in their hearts, the children he has given them or all of life's joys, but also for the progress in their marriage which he brings about through that hard school of mutual understanding.[10]

This is our ideal, but how can a couple begin? We have acknowledged that some spouses are extremely uncomfortable even talking about praying together or having couple devotions. Some things take time to develop. Do not feel pressured by the Arps. But we do challenge you to move out of your comfort zone and be willing to talk about what step you could take to move toward more spiritual intimacy.

The ten-minute miracle. At a recent Marriage Alive seminar, a couple came up to us during one of the breaks. "We've been married for eleven years twice!" the wife told us. "Eleven bad years followed by eleven good years. We actually got remarried."

"Several years ago we paid one thousand dollars to a professional counselor," the husband added, "as we worked through some crisis problems at that time. This prescription was by far the best learning we took away from that interaction. We gladly pass this along to you free of charge and highly recommend it! Praying together daily has changed our relationship at the deepest, most significant and lasting level. God is the miracle worker! Here is our prescription for a marriage miracle."

You can modify this plan and make it your own. The vital ingredient is daily prayer time together!

> Five minutes—Scripture reading
> Two minutes—one prays
> Two minutes—the other prays
> One minute—silence before the Lord
> Monday, Wednesday, Friday—husband takes the lead
> Tuesday, Thursday, Saturday—wife takes the lead
> Sunday—the Lord leads

The Quaker tradition. If you are hesitant to pray out loud with your spouse, you might try the Quaker method of sharing silence. This would allow each of you to worship according to your own personal needs, to seek communion with God separately and privately, yet be supported by the awareness that your spouse is also sharing in the experience. It is an easy first step in worshiping together. According to the Quaker tradition, the devotional time is appropriately concluded with the kiss of peace.[11]

Together Serve Others

As we surmount this spiritual challenge, living out our marriages will serve as a model to others. Remember our cord of three strands in part 1 and how the Holy Spirit helps to hold our strands together and makes us one in him? It is our heavenly Father who gives purpose and meaning not only to our lives but to our marriage. And one way we can serve others is to reflect his image to a hurting world! If you think that is an audacious statement, read Matthew 19:5 and Mark 10:7. In both passages, Jesus reminds us that the Creator made us male and female and created us in God's image. It's a mystery, but some how or another, as husband and wife, together we have the potential to reflect God's image. Your marriage can be a lighthouse.

Chuck Colsen, in *Kingdoms in Conflict*, talks about the church's having little Christian outposts in a world that desperately needs hope.[12] Our marriages should be little beacons that give light to others and create a thirst for healthy marriage relationships.

Your marriage (especially in the second half) can be a lighthouse to a hurting and confused world. Today we need a widespread movement that will produce large numbers of Christian marriages that provide working models of Jesus' teachings about creative love in human relationships. Wouldn't you like to have a part in seeing this happen? You can! The Maces say, "We believe that any married couple, at any stage in their life together, can restructure their relationship to bring it into line with the divine purpose."[13]

Ultimately, our spiritual pilgrimage should lead us to the place of service. In the second half of marriage, we should have more time and opportunity to give to others. It can be a joy to serve others together, when we have a good relationship. And if we successfully surmount this eighth midlife marital challenge, we will have something to pass on to others!

HIS BANNER OVER US IS LOVE

In the first century, the love that the followers of Jesus showed to one another turned the world upside down. Today we have the same potential when we cover our marriages with God's sacred canopy of love. In the end, it is not the form or style of marriage you choose but the love you show to one another and to others that will influence those around you who are looking for hope.

Will you accept our challenge to build your marriage under God's holy, sacred canopy? Not only will you surmount the eight midlife challenges, you will surmount them with your best friend!

❧

MARRIAGE BUILDER

Building Your Sacred Marriage Canopy

1. What are your basic beliefs about what makes a marriage Christian? (You may want to use the Maces' list on pages 176–77 as a discussion starter.)

2. In what ways does your marriage reflect God's image?

3. Individually and as a couple, where are you on your spiritual pilgrimage?

4. How can you promote spiritual closeness with your spouse and with God?

5. How can you serve others?

PART THREE

❧

The Story of
the McCrackens

——— ❧ ———

Now this is the sum of the matter: if ye will be happy
in marriage, confide, love, and be patient; be faithful,
firm, and holy.

—Martin F. Tupper

Meet John and Sarah McCracken

—— ✧ ——

There is no possible doubt that we can have better marriages if we want them enough.

—David and Vera Mace[1]

We want to introduce you to a couple who in midlife had the courage and confidence to make needed changes to grow in their personal life and in their marriage relationship. They are a living example that marital growth can take place at any point of a marriage—even one that has been in neutral for many years.

We met John and Sarah McCracken almost twenty years ago, when they were in their forties and in the middle of parenting adolescents. We still remember the first time we were invited to their house for dinner. When our son, Jonathan, spilled his spaghetti on one of their lovely upholstered dining room chairs, they handled his accident with grace and humor. Here was a family we wanted to know better. The McCrackens were creative and fun to be with. Over the years, we developed a deep and abiding friendship with their whole family.

John is a surgeon. Sarah was a full-time mom. Their three children were creative, independent, and completely different from each other. The first half of the McCrackens' marriage went according to plan. John worked hard and provided abundantly for his family while keeping up his golfing skills. Sarah enjoyed the challenge of providing the environment for growth for her children, and participated in book clubs and other community and church activities. All in all, quite a typical, traditional American marriage.

The second half of marriage has been another story! They were thoroughly unprepared for the changes and challenges ahead of them. But they are a living example of what we have been talking about for the last eight chapters. Over the past decade, we watched as they overcame many struggles to surmount the challenges of all long-term marriages.

In the process, they moved from a more conventional marriage to a companionship marriage. Now they are best friends and close companions. But it wasn't without risk, hard work, determination—and some pain. Over the years, they kept a journal of their pilgrimage into the second half of marriage. Now they share their story to encourage you and give you hope. We have changed their names, but their story is genuine and heartwarming. In the coming pages, we'll let them tell you their own story.

JOHN MCCRACKEN'S WAKE-UP CALL

"I prided myself on how well I provided for my family and how esteemed I was in the medical community," began John McCracken. "Why, I was on five different boards, chief of staff of our local hospital, chairman of my church's missions committee, one of the best golfers in town, and well respected in the community. Sure I was a workaholic, but what I didn't realize was that I was working myself right out of my family. My wake-up call came on a family vacation in Europe.

"I was forty-six, Sarah was forty-four, and our three children were twenty-one, nineteen, and fifteen. Our older daughter and son were in college, and our younger daughter was in high school. This was to be the vacation of vacations. Now that the children were older, it should have been a wonderful family time. My sense that all was not well began soon after we arrived in England. Somehow I just didn't get the family jokes. It seemed Sarah and the children had an inside line to each other, and I was on the outside, tagging along and picking up the bills. I watched while the other four in our family had fun together. I felt invisible and definitely on the outside looking in."

WHO'S GOT THE GARBAGE?

"It all came to a head one day when we stopped in the lake district for a picnic. After we finished eating, everyone (but me) wanted to walk on up the path to the top of a hill to see the view. Why didn't I want to join them? It all had to do with the garbage. There was no trash can, and I didn't want to leave the garbage behind. Our son said, 'Oh Dad, don't worry about it; we'll come right back by here to the car, and we can pick it up then.'

"'No!' I said. I thought we should carry it with us. After another round of verbal missiles, Sarah and the children simply left me holding the garbage while they walked on up the path to see the view. There I sat by myself with the garbage, wondering how I had lost control of my family. Sarah was connected to the kids, and I was not. I wasn't even part of the McCracken clan! And I had worked so hard for them. It was my hard work that provided this great vacation! No one seemed to appreciate me.

"After sulking in my misery, I began to realize that professional success—even being at the top of my profession—just wasn't fulfilling. Medicine is a jealous god, but I began to realize that it wasn't more important than my family. For me it was a real moment of truth. I didn't know my family, but I desperately wanted to. For the next couple of weeks in Europe, I was able to step out of the rat race and get reacquainted with the McCracken family.

"During this trip, we spent a week with the Arps, who then lived in Vienna, Austria. There I began to relax. Each morning, Claudia served us breakfast on the balcony, and we would sit for hours over coffee and just enjoy talking and being. It was a totally new experience for this driven doctor!

"That was over fifteen years ago, but it seems like yesterday. Change isn't easy, but I can tell you by experience, it is possible. And it didn't happen overnight. In the next years, as our children left the nest, were married, and began their own families, we still had miles to go. Old hurts and issues had to be faced."

SARAH MCCRACKEN'S RESPONSE

"I was shocked when John actually relaxed and began to slow down and focus a little more on our family and me," Sarah McCracken said. "Frankly, it made me uncomfortable. We made it through the first twenty-five years of our marriage with a comfortable but rather distant relationship. While we didn't have a lot of closeness, I always considered our marriage above average. Actually, looking back, I'd have to say both of us took our marriage for granted—and that made transitional times in our marriage a little scary.

"When I met John, I knew he was the independent type, and that was fine with me—I also liked my space. We knew our roles and played them with skill and harmony. Most of the time, we got the job done with poise and grace. John provided abundantly for our family, and I prided myself by pursuing parenting with the same dedication I would have if I had been a corporate executive. I never resented being the chief nurturer and considered myself one of the truly liberated women who enjoyed being a professional mom.

"So when our younger daughter, Claire, left for college in the early eighties, it was a real change for me. At first it was as if I had been hit by a ten-ton truck—I was devastated! I was out of a job. So being the independent type, I started to look around for opportunities for growth. I am a very intense person, extremely interested in the world around me; I needed something to pour my energy into. I never gave much consideration to pouring that energy into my marriage—the independent doctor was unlikely to really change. But as our nest emptied, John began to show more interest in getting reacquainted.

"So we began to look around to see what we had in common. One of the first things we did (a little under duress) was go through the Arps' first book on marriage, *Ten Dates for Mates*. We even threw a little celebration for Dave and Claudia on the occasion of the publication of their first book, so we felt obligated to read through it. One thing we discovered was that we really didn't know each other very well, and in some ways never had.

"I do remember one of our 'ten dates.' We walked several miles to a downtown restaurant and back. The main thing I remember from that experience was my hurting feet! But we did begin to try out a few things as a couple.

"Our first project was to buy a condo at the beach. After all, we had 'arrived'—our children were launched, John was a successful surgeon—and we deserved it. Or so we thought. John is an avid golfer, so Myrtle Beach, South Carolina, with its many golf courses, was a perfect location for him! I like to read, putter around through the shops, and walk on the beach. It sounded like a dream come true, but it didn't work out that way. It actually became a nightmare. I developed an allergy to the sun that only affected me at Myrtle Beach! Since the sun shines most of the time there, I felt like a prisoner in our beach condo.

"While the condo didn't work very well for us, it worked great for our married children and friends. The Arps even wrote a couple of books there. But all in all, I'd have to say this was one project that didn't work out. It did reveal our determination to reconnect, but later we discovered we each had a different perspective of how close we wanted that connection to be."

THE MCCRACKENS MUSTER UP THE COURAGE TO CHANGE

"When our daughter, Claire, left for college, it wasn't only Sarah who was out of pocket," said John McCracken. "Our daughter was a classical guitarist, and I can't tell you how much I missed hearing her play. Our house was entirely too quiet. Hearing her play the guitar had been therapy for both of us.

"The lack of depth in my relationship with my family became even more pronounced in my relationship with Sarah now that Claire was gone. The condo at the beach just moved our lack of contentment three hundred miles east. We hit an emotional void, and it took years to work through it. I lost my motivation for work. We'd spent the first half of our marriage raising our family and getting established in my profession. Now I questioned why I was working eighty-hour weeks. The kids were gone. Money—what is it for? Why was I working so hard? We were successful by the world's standards, but something was missing."

"John and I really didn't have much to say to each other," Sarah said. "Frankly, we were bored. I think that's one reason we bought the beach condo. And then there was our swimming pool in the backyard. The pool that over the years provided so much family fun was now empty. I wanted to fill it in and plant a rose garden. John stubbornly said, 'No!' He didn't want to let it go. Forget the fact that he never used it. He was like the ostrich that put his head in sand—he just didn't want his life to change. Yet that swimming pool was a daily reminder that life had changed. Soon that was another subject we never talked about!

"I began to seriously consider what I wanted to do with the rest of my life—not necessarily in tandem with John's plans. I'm an activist and a survivor, so I began to consider different options. For a time I thought the solution was to adopt a refugee family. John agreed to go along with me, and we pursued it for about a year, but it never worked out. We would get right down to the week when the family was going to show up, and then for some reason their arrival was canceled—this occurred three times."

"While the refugee family never arrived, getting ready for them precipitated us mustering up the courage to change," John said. "We were going to put them in our basement apartment, and I remember one day going through boxes of golf trophies and throwing them out."

"Now, this was scary," Sarah said. "Golf is John's chief joy in life. The trophies confirmed that he was a very, very good golfer and that he was very, very competitive. And now he was throwing his trophies away.

"So we began to talk to each other. One of the first things we discovered was that the second half of marriage is a very personal stage of life, and neither of us handled the personal side of life very well. When the kids leave home, you are left only with each other. In a long discussion with John, we were talking about what we wanted most for the rest of our life, and John surprised me by saying, 'Sarah, I want our marriage to be better!'

"I was totally shocked! This was the man who wanted freedom and space, and now he was saying he wanted intimacy. This was too much for me to really comprehend. It's like, you think you really know someone, and then you realize you don't know that person at all. Since when was he so concerned about our marriage?"

"I know I shocked Sarah," John continued, "but after much introspection, that's what I really wanted. I wanted our marriage to be better, and I was willing to do whatever it took to make it happen. I wanted a closer relationship with Sarah. I wanted us to be able to talk in a personal way.

"Sarah's response was, 'We can do it, but it will cost you!' It did cost both of us, but the emotional closeness we have achieved over the past ten years is well worth it! But it wasn't easy."

THE MCCRACKENS LEARN NEW SKILLS

"During the first half of our marriage," said Sarah, "here's the way we communicated: John was distant and avoided conflict and deep conversations. I was more intrusive and liked to confront issues head-on. It was as if we were on opposite sides of a continuum."

"It was easy for me to live in my own little world," John explained. "I could tune everything out. Sarah was a wonderful mother and manager, so I didn't have to be concerned about things on the home front. When Sarah would confront me, I would retreat even more.

"Perhaps I rationalized—after all, we had a 'medical marriage.' Communication and intimacy often play smaller roles in the lives of doctors and their spouses. It wasn't that we disagreed more than other couples. It was more as if we lived parallel lives with separate goals, concerns, hopes, and joys. Face it, anyone who works twelve-hour-plus days is probably going to be exhausted at the end of the day. And when you're tired, heart-to-heart conversations just don't tend to happen— at least, that was true in our experience.

"In the first half of marriage, your marriage has a rhythm. You get married; then you have children. You work hard building your career. The children start school, and family life centers around the myriad of kids' activities. Add birthdays, holidays, family vacations, graduations— they all promote a familiar hectic routine and provide plenty of things to talk about.

"Then the second half of marriage comes around, and it catches you totally off guard. My aloofness that previously worked now revealed an emotional separation from Sarah. I felt alone, totally outside our relationship—that's one reason I wanted us to work on our marriage. I just didn't know how to start talking about it."

Sarah said, "John often told me I was the family pusher, and that was basically how I communicated with John for the first half of our marriage. It was easy for me to get into this mode. I was the one to see that teeth got brushed, homework done, beds made, and that the kids got to soccer practice and music lessons on time.

"It naturally followed that I helped organize John. 'Honey, the Johnsons are coming for an early dinner on Saturday. Please plan to get home a little earlier from your golf game than you did last week.' And so life went!"

"The problem arose when we hit midlife," John said, "and life wasn't so black-and-white. The success ladder was not so attractive from the top looking down. I began to think about my life and realized my marriage meant a lot to me and I wanted to make it a priority, even if it meant I'd have to sacrifice and give up a little of me. That's about the time we had that intensive conversation about making our marriage better and we both realized we would have to change.

"So we renewed our commitment to growing together in our marriage and began to work on our communication. We began to make ourselves more vulnerable to each other, and—though very hard for me—we began to express our inner feelings."

DEALING WITH THEIR DIFFERENCES

"For the first half of our marriage, we basically ignored conflict," John said. "Our marriage was more conventional. We had our somewhat rigid roles but did a good job of balancing them and staying out of each other's hair. At times, we got upset with each other, but we functioned. No great conflict, but no great closeness either."

Sarah added, "John's right. He was more of a benevolent dictator, but he basically steered clear of my domain. Decisions concerning home and family were usually mine. The only time this created tension was the years we were in a very conservative group that pushed male leadership. John simply didn't need that reinforcement! When I deferred to him to make decisions in my areas of expertise, he began to lose respect for me, and I became impatient with his dumb decisions. I was told that if I treated him as 'king,' I would be 'queen,' but it didn't happen that way. Frankly, it just didn't work very well for us, so slowly we gave each other more space and reverted to more distance in our relationship, and our old patterns and roles.

"But when we entered the second half of our marriage and tried to build a closer, more personal and equal style of marriage, then the sparks began to fly! The closer we tried to draw to each other, the more issues surfaced, but we weren't sure how to handle them.

"Over the years I was the talker. I would talk, talk, talk, but never get around to acting. John would smile, look interested, but on the inside he could just tune me out.

"Before our daughter's wedding, my big project was remodeling our old English Tudor home. At this point, our level of teamwork was that I made most of the choices and decisions, and John provided the finances. That was until we came to the issue of redecorating our bedroom. Going all the way back to my childhood, I loved hardwood floors. I discovered that under the carpet in our bedroom were beautiful hardwood floors just waiting to be restored.

"The only problem was that John preferred carpeting. I talked, talked, and talked. I pleaded—you could almost say I begged—for the hardwood floors. At last there was a breakthrough. John agreed. I could hardly believe I had won this battle. Actually, I hadn't. The night before the workmen were to come to pull up the carpets and start on the floors, John called them and canceled the job. He simply changed his mind. He just couldn't give in.

"All the anger of all of the years of our marriage energized me the next day! If he wouldn't listen to my words, maybe he would respect my actions. Single-handedly I ripped up the carpeting in our bedroom. Hardwood floors—they weren't pretty but I had them! And at last I had John's attention!"

John agreed. "Sarah definitely got my attention! For the first time, I listened to her and actually respected the fact that she did something about her frustration with me. I realized that if we were going to renew our marriage and make it better, it would only happen as we worked together. I had to give up being a benevolent dictator, and I had to give up some of my autonomy.

"On that day, together we reached a compromise. We recarpeted our bedroom. Sarah got her hardwood floors in the home we built in the mountains. But that's getting ahead of our story. But what we learned at this point in our marriage was that we didn't have to keep trying to get our own way. We could work things out together."

THE MCCRACKENS MAKE BIG DECISIONS

"Frankly, at this point we felt over our heads," said John, "as we worked on our marriage of forty-plus years. But the carpet episode got my attention. I became much more observant. One day, I even noticed Sarah was reading a book entitled *Creative Divorce*, and I must say that made me very uncomfortable. Why was she reading that, when I had so clearly expressed I wanted us to have a better marriage? I guess I hadn't really understood her answer, 'It will cost you.' I was now ready to understand."

"John's attitude did change," Sarah continued, "and I sensed he really was serious about improving our relationship. But it was going to cost both of us! First, we both had to give up a little of our individuality and independence to forge a companionship marriage. Second, it was going to cost us time and energy, and later when we chose a common project to learn how to work together, it was going to cost us financially!

"He was really nervous when he saw that book on divorce. I have always been an inquisitive person. From my years at Duke University, I learned to explore the possibilities and exhaust the possibilities. I prided myself in being intellectually self-reliant, so I decided to learn all I could about marriage—including what causes divorce. My goal was to avoid it.

"But now I had the doctor's attention. I remember him asking me what step he could take to improve our relationship. My answer was simple: 'Read one book on marriage!'"

"She didn't tell me which book to read," John said, "so I went to the bookstore and started looking through the various books on marriage. I shudder to think how disastrous this could have been—to pick out one book among all the different philosophies and approaches to marriage and base my actions upon that one book! Now I know there is a personal God who cares for his people and leads them in unusual ways, for on this day, totally out of ignorance, I picked out just the book I needed! It was a book written by Gary Smalley, entitled *If Only He Knew*. The title made sense to me, because if there was something I needed to know about Sarah and our marriage, I wanted to learn whatever I needed to know.

"In the book was a self-test to see how competent you are concerning your marriage. I took the test and I flunked it! That was an eye-opener—a milestone in our marriage. We began to talk more in-depth with each other about our relationship, and I really tried to understand things from Sarah's perspective.

"At this point, we realized that we never had learned how to work together. Sarah suggested we choose a project that we could do together—one that would be of equal interest to both of us, and something we both felt passionate about."

Sarah smiled as she said, "Here is where John began to realize just how much this was going to cost him! Remember the beach condo that didn't work out? Well, for years we had also enjoyed vacationing in western North Carolina. Actually, when we were college students, we met each other at a mountain resort where we both had summer jobs. So it was a good compromise for us. There were lots of great golf courses for John, and the North Carolina sun and I got along just fine. We decided to build a home there for our pleasure now and retirement later. Now remember, we had never done anything like this before! We knew we would enjoy a mountain home, but our real goal was to build a partnership and learn to cooperate and work together. Talk about risks! We took them! But I hate to think where we would be today if we had not decided to risk growing together.

"There's a quote I found that describes how we felt as we began to take risks for our marriage to grow: 'It's a risk, you know—more than that which we took on our wedding day many years ago. We pledged ourselves to stay together in the face of hardships we could understand: sickness, tight budgets, disappointments. But deepening the meaning of our marriage is a call to venture into uncharted waters. With a prayer for courage, let's begin.'"[2]

THE MCCRACKENS SEARCH FOR MEANING

"Working to renew our marriage," Sarah said, "led us to think more about our individual selves and the meaning of life in general. I noticed that many of my friends were making drastic changes in their lives. It was a little scary, and I wanted to make sure that if I did make changes, they would be the reasonable ones. About this time, John's mother gave me some excellent advice.

"She observed that among the social or country club set, age forty-nine to fifty was a very dangerous time, and she had observed a disastrous pattern. With youthfulness fleeting away, some women lost ten pounds, got a new wardrobe, a new job, and a new life. They felt young, good, free, and that the world was theirs for the taking. They went into business, got rid of old husbands, and some found new husbands. No one was going to hold them down or keep them from being all they could be.

"What they didn't realize was that in ten years they would be sixty. They would be senior citizens. Then they would realize that they had given up everything for ten years. Everything they needed at sixty they got rid of at fifty. They threw it all away, and regardless of what they looked like or felt like at fifty, they're now sixty.

"Well, that showed me what I didn't want to do. But what were my interests? What was my passion in life? Before discovering what our couple passion was, I needed to know my own. I decided to take an inventory of my interests. Here is my list:

travel—museums, crafts, culture, plays, and so on;

church—teaching children, Bible study, Sunday school, fellowship, special small groups;
home—architecture, upkeep, entertaining;
family—everything;
reading—Bible study, southern authors, biography, psychology;
entertainment—plays, eating out."

"Sarah really got into trying to figure out her passion for life, and what her interests were," John said, "so she encouraged me to do the same. I always saw medicine as my first career, but it was not all I wanted to do in life. Even before we were married, we talked about retirement, and I always told Sarah I wanted to retire early and do something else. I'm still trying to discover what that something else is. For a time, I thought I wanted to have a second career in medical ethics, and I even enrolled in a Ph.D. program at the university. But after a couple of courses that weren't that challenging, I lost interest. I've always been interested in missions and presently am on the board of a medical benevolence ministry. I would like to go to a third-world country and work, but at this point Sarah wouldn't even consider it! Her idea of roughing it is a night at the Hilton. I didn't have the big picture, but I could start, like Sarah did, and make a list of my interests. You'll probably observe how different our lists are:

travel—sightseeing, history;
home—beauty, comfort;
golf—everywhere;
work—medical practice, investing;
church—fellowship, charity, missions;
reading—sports, theology, philosophy, money management.

"We tried to think of interests we had in common, and at first all we could think of was that we both liked to eat at nice restaurants! After much effort, we came up with the following common ground:

eating out;
walking together;
travel—nongolfing (we did like to attend educational seminars);

entertainment—plays, musicals, shopping;

Bible study, church;

our North Carolina project—real estate, home improvement."

"It wasn't long after we made out our list," Sarah continued, "that we had the opportunity to attend an educational seminar at our alma mater, Duke University. It was entitled 'Search for Meaning,' and that was what we were searching for. I have always liked intellectual stimulation. Gail Sheehy was one of the speakers, and all in all I found it a very good experience. It was a catalyst to reexamining our past as it relates to our future.

"On the way home I asked John to tell me about his life—starting when he was a little boy—and I offered to write down his life story. The husband who rarely talks about himself spent the first 150 miles telling me about his life from age one to seven. For the first time, I began to understand this man I had been living with all these years, and he began to better understand himself. For instance, I'd never realized the impact of the Vietnam War. The week before John's thirty-fifth birthday, he was drafted into the army! We were stationed at El Paso, Texas. Those years, from my perspective, were good ones. John didn't have to go to Vietnam. He came home earlier than in his private practice. We did more things together as a family. I had no real complaints! But for John, it was a totally different experience."

John said, "I never brought my work home with me, so Sarah never knew the physical devastation I saw every day. Many of the soldiers wounded in Vietnam were flown to the Army Medical Center at El Paso. As a surgeon, I was involved in reconstructive surgery on mangled young men who would never live normal lives again. What was the purpose of all of this? War is insane and inhuman, and I was caught up in one of the ugliest parts of it. When I came home, I wanted to escape, and that's what I did."

"As the miles went by and John continued to pour out his heart," Sarah told us, "something wonderful began to happen: we were being knit together as one in a totally new and deeper way. Life took on a deeper meaning. Things mattered much less. We have had two major robberies—our silver and many of our other wedding presents are history. Matthew 6:19–21 has taken on new meaning for us: 'Do not store up for yourselves treasures on earth, where moth and rust destroy, and where thieves break in and steal. But store up for yourselves treasures in heaven, where moth and rust do not destroy, and where thieves do not break in and steal. For where your treasure is, there your heart will be also.' Our relationship became one of our most precious treasures. At last we were best friends and close companions."

"At this point, we began cutting loose of some of the things that had gripped us in the past," said John. "We began to experiment and try new things. But the really positive thing was that we were doing it together! At last we were learning to cooperate and work together. It's time now to tell you about our mountain venture."

A HOME IN THE MOUNTAINS

"After our beach condo disaster," Sarah said, "we wanted to go slow in pursuing other real estate adventures, so it literally took us years to decide to build a home in the North Carolina mountains. However, this was different from anything we had ever done in the past. We chose this project to build our marriage. From the start, it was a couple passion—we wanted to learn how to work together, how to cooperate, and how to become closer companions. Our vehicle was our building project."

"Basically, we only made decisions when we both agreed," John continued. "This was totally different from my approach to things in the past. I was committed to Sarah and to deciding things together. This was not to be a 'pumpkin house,' like in the nursery rhyme:

Peter, Peter, pumpkin eater
Had a wife but couldn't keep her;
Put her in a pumpkin shell
And there he kept her very well.

"While in the past I had been more of a Peter-style husband, now I was totally reformed! It wasn't just what I wanted or desired. This house was to express our creativity and style as a couple. Yes, I even decided that wood floors for a large part of our house would be 'us.'"

"It took over a year for our house to be built," Sarah said. "We didn't do the actual construction work, but we were involved in most all of the decisions. Actually, we weren't in a hurry, and we never forgot that this wasn't about building a house; it was about building our marriage. I can honestly say that our house project, while a tremendous challenge to both of us, was one of the best steps we ever took to forge a closer relationship. Through this experience, not only did we come to know each other better, we came to know ourselves as well. We had reached our second adulthood. We had begun our second marriage!"

During this time, we watched John and Sarah begin to change. They were like two kids. They were so excited about their "couple project." We knew how special this was to them when one evening as we were together at their home, they showed us a model of the house they were building. They'd actually had someone construct a miniature model of their home! But the most interesting thing to us was the new closeness we began to notice in their relationship.

They really seemed to enjoy being together. We asked them, "So much of what you have shared with us is really 'heavy stuff.' What kinds of things do you do just for fun?"

THE MCCRACKENS DISCOVER TWO-PART FUN

Sarah told us, "We are trying to put more fun in our lives. And to do the unexpected is a great boredom preventer. For instance, last Tuesday morning I was out shopping, and it was close to lunchtime. I usually swing by home and have a bowl of soup with carrot sticks or some other reasonable, healthy lunch. But on this day, I went by the doughnut shop and bought two jelly doughnuts. I took them home and ate them for lunch. It definitely inserted humor in our day when I later told John what I had done!"

"I guess now the McCrackens have become less predictable," John told us, "but life is definitely becoming more pleasurable for both of us.

I still can't visualize health-conscious Sarah downing two jelly dough-nuts for lunch! As we told you previously, when we first started look-ing for what we had in common, the only thing we both agreed on was that we both liked to go out to eat together. But that started the process of looking for other things we could do together to put more fun in our relationship. Of course, building our home in North Carolina was our major couple project, but along the way, we discovered little out-of-the-way places for eating and entertainment. We even discovered they have an annual 'woolly worm' race, which we attended.

"We were both interested in our ancestry, so we began to explore our roots. On one trip to Europe, we found the little Irish village where the McCrackens came from, and recently, on our way to the Arps' youngest son's wedding, we took a side trip to Missouri to find where Sarah's father's family came from. We even found the little church her great-grandfather pastored!"

"Now, we don't have to do all the fun things together," Sarah said. "John's golfing remains a big part of his recreational life. And I've dis-covered interests of my own. A couple of years ago I decided to take lessons in watercolor painting. Also, I developed an interest in decora-tive folk art and persuaded John to travel off the beaten track looking for treasures. Another interest I have is putting together family scrap-books. I try to choose a theme and make them creative. Literally, I can spend days doing this!"

"Let me add," John said, "developing shared interests has not been a snap for us. It took time and real commitment. But is has been a key element in making our marriage better."

THE MCCRACKENS DISCOVER THE ESSENCE OF LOVE

"When you asked us to share our story with you," John told us, "you caused us to do a wonderful thing. Reviewing the last decade of our lives helped us look closely at our marriage as it was then and now. We have been involved in a ten-year process of developing emotional closeness. It has not been an easy or quick process for us and has been time intensive, with no shortcuts.

"But we are amazed at our perspective now! We have restructured our relationship, and we sincerely believe it is more aligned with God's purpose for our lives. We have become close companions and best friends. Our marriage today is more important to both of us than our individual wants and desires.

"Over these ten years, we have experienced growing together spiritually. The two main areas we worked on and have progressed in are forgiveness and pride. During the first half of our marriage, we kept anger down, but we didn't really talk on the personal level that we do now. Before, I never took Sarah seriously. Now we can talk on the most personal level. We've worked through forgiving each other as well as other people in our lives. Sarah had to forgive me and come to peace with her own self. *Forgiveness* had to become a way of life.

"Pride was my problem. I wanted to be all things to all people. It's easy, as a medical doctor, to have a 'messiah' complex. We want to cure everyone's problems. I was proud of my accomplishments, but not only in my profession but in my golfing and community service, and we did have a wonderful family. Speaking of golfing, I really think that in the first half of our marriage, I used golfing to vent my emotions, rather than making myself vulnerable to Sarah, and that was a barrier to building emotional closeness in our relationship.

"I wanted to be perfect and have the perfect marriage. But in the past few years, I've also come to be at peace with myself and my imperfections and have a healthier and more realistic self-concept. When I gave up the idea of a perfect marriage, I began to realize we could have a growing one. But the turning point was when we began to understand ourselves. This helped us to understand each other.

"After striving for the past ten years to renew our marriage, I have come to this conclusion—the essence of love is trying to understand your mate! The degree to which you understand your mate can determine the level of love you have toward your spouse. And the more we understand each other, the more we love each other, the more oneness and spiritual unity we can achieve. That's the goal of marriage. And now I understand what I meant when I said to Sarah, 'I want us to have a better marriage!'"

A LETTER FROM THE MCCRACKENS

As we were completing our manuscript for this book, we received a letter from John and Sarah. In a winsome way, they summarized their progress in surmounting the challenges of building a better marriage and a closer relationship for the second half of their marriage. Their letter encouraged us, and we hope it will also encourage you.

January 1996

Dear Claudia and Dave,

Happy New Year! The holidays have passed very quickly and very busily, and we have failed to write our traditional Christmas cards and letters. With apologies, we wish you a belated Merry Christmas and Happy New Year. We are having a wonderful time in the mountains, and the snow is beautiful. Wish you were here!

We missed being in our old home, close enough to share a bit of your Austrian Christmas celebration. We missed reminiscing about Christmases past, when our family travels brought us together. We missed sharing all the latest pictures of our children and grandchildren, but there will be time for that later.

In reviewing our thoughts on our forty years of marriage, we asked ourselves what discoveries we felt we'd made, what we'd learned, and how we feel as we close this chapter of our life and begin our adventure into retirement. By far, the biggest discovery was that we *should* change and *could* change! At first change was very threatening, but when we became involved and discovered we could, it became very exciting.

Next we had to relearn how to listen to each other, the most important step in any communication. Becoming better listeners, being more honest, more careful, and more companionable, we learned much about ourselves and each other. Also, learning to work together, we developed more trust and reliance on each other.

Finally, we feel we have reshaped, reworked, and reformed our marriage relationship, in a manner compatible with this stage of life. We look forward to the next chapter in our life together with great optimism and enthusiasm.

In closing we want you to know how much we appreciate your encouragement. With marriage and family values being stressed in today's Christian communities, it is amazing how little is being done about it. We pray God will be with you, guide you, and bless you in your work in this much needed arena.

Best of friends,
John and Sarah

Our message to you is simple: We want you to have a better marriage. We want the second half of your marriage to outshine the first half. We want to give you new hope, to challenge you to rediscover the true purpose and meaning of life. We want you to reestablish your relationship, like the McCrackens have done, and be closer than you ever thought possible. It is now up to you. Will your accept the challenge? If your answer is yes, then you have the potential to make the rest of your marriage the best.

PART FOUR

❧

The Marriage Challenge

———— ❧ ————

Then, whatever weather come, or shine, or shade,
We'll set out together, not a whit afraid.
Age is ne'er alarming—I shall find, I ween,
You at sixty charming as at sweet sixteen.

—D. M. M. Craik

Challenge Your Marriage

Courageous risks are life giving, they help you grow, make you brave and better than you think you are.

—Marie Curie

One of the major challenges of the second half of marriage is dealing with change. When we made a move from our family home to our condo, one change we gladly accepted was having someone else do our yard work.

We just love Tuesdays, when the yard crew comes through and spit-shines our yard! But where we live, if you want more trees and extra shrubs, you have to take care of planting them yourself. No problem. We have a friend, Robert, who is handy in the yard and who agreed to help us plant some more trees and shrubbery. We were leaving for a conference, so he said just to leave our shrubs and trees in the yard where we wanted them and he would plant them while we were gone. *How clever,* we thought.

It was early fall, so we decided to leave our indoor ficus tree out on our deck for one more trip. It's a temperamental plant that lives inside in the winter and almost dies. Then we put it on our deck for the summer, and it gets healthy again. So one last week out for Mr. Ficus Tree.

We did not count on a storm to race through Knoxville while we were gone. We even lost two large trees in our front yard. After the storm, Robert came to plant the new trees and shrubs. They were somewhat in the area we wanted them, but the funny thing that happened was that the ficus tree got planted by the steps to our deck. It had blown off the deck in the storm, and Robert, seeing it by the steps, put that baby in the ground. Let us tell you, it was well planted!

The ficus plant is a tropical plant, and the prognosis for it surviving a Knoxville winter was not good. So after several more weeks of glorying in the fall sunshine—and, we might add, thriving—our little tree was uprooted and relocated to a larger planter than it had originally. After a few days of acclimating, it was brought inside. So far, it's doing great! Being uprooted and replanted was like a shot of vitamins for our little tree.

Why are we telling you this story? Because it illustrates what we hope will happen to your marriage as you finish this book. This is a book about making the rest of your marriage the best. It's about the second half of your marriage—a time of change and challenges. It can be a time of uprooting negative habits and replacing them with more healthy ones. It can be a time of replanting a root-bound marriage in healthy soil that will cause it to grow with vigor and zest. But it won't happen without effort on your part.

LOOKING BACK: THE LAST DECADE OF MARRIAGE

Life rushes by. In each passing decade, time seems to accelerate. The less of life there is to waste, the more precious it becomes. The second half of marriage is full of changes, but while change is inevitable, growth is optional.

Think about the last decade of your marriage. What changes have you experienced? In the last decade, our sons left the nest, graduated from college, met and married their wives. Ten years ago our sons were financially dependent on us. Now they are financially on their own. (Yes!) We have said our earthly good-byes to two of our parents and hello to three grandchildren. We have moved from our family home into our condo house, and our lifestyle has changed from basically being at home to being on the road much of the time. A decade ago we were getting ready for a big family Christmas at our house. This past Christmas, we gathered for the holidays at our son's home in Virginia.

LOOKING AHEAD: THE NEXT DECADE OF MARRIAGE

Changes—they come to us all. What will the next decade hold? A decade from now our grandchildren will almost be teenagers, and we will be in our sixties! In a decade, we won't be retired, but we will probably be able to see it from there. What will our marriage look like ten years from now? We know that if we want to continue to grow our marriage, we will have to adjust to change.

In part 1, we told you about how we met the Maces and discovered a marriage model we wanted to follow. Over the years, they encouraged us and helped us to become close companions in our marriage relationship, and we have attempted to pass on some of their wisdom to you. They emphasized the importance of adjusting to change when they wrote,

> Marriage is an almost endless series of adjustments between two people—adjustments to each other and to the ever-changing circumstances of human life. But the rewards fully justify the effort. A truly happy and successful marriage is the best-known guarantee of lifelong happiness.[1]

CHALLENGING YOUR MARRIAGE FOR THE SECOND HALF

Are you willing to risk change to enhance your marriage? Are you willing to develop new habits to foster positive change? Psychologists tell us it takes three weeks to make a new habit, and six weeks to feel comfortable about it. As we work with couples, so many times we see that it's not a matter of knowing what to do but doing what we know. It is up to you to define what you are going to do in the next weeks, months, and years to enrich your marriage and move it from better to best.

The key part of our six-hour Marriage Alive seminar is what happens after the seminar is over. We usually lead our seminar in the context of a church, and most of the time, the couples form supper clubs after the seminar. With several other couples, they meet together once a month for four months. They go back over the material we covered in our seminar and work through a Bible study on each topic. Besides their monthly dinners, they agree to have a date with their mate between each dinner. Plus, the couples hold each other accountable and encourage each other to grow in their marriage.

You could use this book in the same way. Call some couple friends who are in or about to enter the second half of marriage, and form your own supper club.

OUR MARRIAGE JOURNEY

One benefit of working on this book has been reflecting on our own marriage of thirty-three-plus years. As we read the surveys, our own marriage was challenged. We became more introspective, and our passion to build our own relationship grew with each response the mailman brought or with each survey our fax machine spit out.

Through the kaleidoscope of over five hundred survey responses, we saw pictures of many unique marriages. Some were beautiful to behold: healthy, loving, warm relationships. Others were distressful: hurting, painful, isolated, and lonely. Most were somewhere on the continuum between ecstasy and despair. We've looked at marriages with no makeup or sugarcoating. The reality of how hard relationships are to maintain has been our constant companion.

We wept with those who were hurting, rejoiced with those who were celebrating healthy, happy relationships, and laughed with those who shared their humor. With each, we were deeply moved to continue in our work to help couples prepare for and surmount the challenges of the second half of marriage. And along with you, we have pursued the eight midlife challenges.

But let us be quick to say that no one—and most of all the Arps— does everything right! You may know all there is to know about marriage enrichment, but that is not a passport to marital success. It's the daily grinding it out. Making unselfish choices, forgiving and asking for forgiveness, and giving each other grace—that's what helps us maintain a healthy marriage. It's choosing daily to grow together.

CHOOSING TO GROW

"If you play it safe in life," says Shirley Hufstedler, "you've decided that you don't want to grow anymore." But the secret of growing is getting started. We suggest that you start by choosing a couple of areas to work on. It's great if you can do this as a couple, but if for some reason you are reading this book alone, choose something you know you can do to improve your marriage relationship, and start there.

Remember, marriage is a journey, not a destination—and no one ever arrives. On our journey, we sometimes do really absurd things, like planting our indoor ficus tree in our yard. But it is as we attempt growth that we make progress and have the potential for growing closer together. Along the way, we will all have our "ficus trees" that we will need to uproot and replant. But it's encouraging to know that even our mistakes can shake us out of complacency and jump-start growth. Our healthy ficus tree is a living example.

And what did the Arps do with the hole vacated by our ficus tree? We found a more appropriate holly shrub to take it's place, but each time we see it, it reminds us of our ficus tree's days in the sun. It reminds us to never give up adventure. To take the risk to grow and, rather than fold our wings, to spread them wide and continue to challenge our marriage with opportunities for growth.

Close to our new holly shrub is a little wooden plaque with one of our favorite quotes, which hopefully describes the future of our marriage. Actually, we began this book with the same quote. It can describe your future, too, if you're willing to challenge your marriage!

> Grow old along with me. The best is yet to be;
> The last of life, for which the first was made.
> Our times are in His hand who saith, "A whole I planned,
> Youth shows but half; Trust God: See all, nor be afraid!"
>
> —Robert Browning

✺

MARRIAGE BUILDER

Challenging Your Marriage

Our challenge to you is to discuss the eight marital challenges. You can use the following three questions to kick off your discussion. You goal is to evaluate where you are, where you would like to be, and what steps you need to take too improve your relationship in each of the eight areas. The three questions are:

1. What evidence is there that we are growing in this area?
2. What evidence is there that we still need to grow in this area?
3. What can I personally do to help us meet this challenge?

The eight marital challenges for the second half of marriage are:

1. Let go of past marital disappointments, forgive each other, and commit to making the rest of your marriage the best.
2. Create a marriage that is partner-focused rather than child-focused.
3. Maintain an effective communication system that allows you to express your deepest feelings, joys, and concerns.
4. Use anger and conflict in a creative way to build your relationship.
5. Build a deeper friendship and enjoy your spouse.
6. Renew romance and restore a pleasurable sexual relationship.
7. Adjust to changing roles with aging parents and adult children.
8. Evaluate where you are on your spiritual pilgrimage, grow closer to each other and to God, and together serve others.

Appendixes

Surveying Your Marriage

Surveying the Second Half of Marriage

Check your level of satisfaction in the following general categories as they relate to your marriage:

Areas of satisfaction or dissatisfaction:

	very dissatisfied			neither			very satisfied		
	1	2	3	4	5	6	7	8	9	10
Financial management	—	—	—	—	—	—	—	—	—	—
Companionship	—	—	—	—	—	—	—	—	—	—
Spiritual growth and commitment	—	—	—	—	—	—	—	—	—	—
Mutual activities	—	—	—	—	—	—	—	—	—	—
Individual activities	—	—	—	—	—	—	—	—	—	—
Communication with mate	—	—	—	—	—	—	—	—	—	—
My health and physical fitness	—	—	—	—	—	—	—	—	—	—
Mate's health and physical fitness	—	—	—	—	—	—	—	—	—	—
Ministry activities	—	—	—	—	—	—	—	—	—	—
Friends and extended family	—	—	—	—	—	—	—	—	—	—
Community service	—	—	—	—	—	—	—	—	—	—
Romance and intimacy	—	—	—	—	—	—	—	—	—	—
Household responsibilities	—	—	—	—	—	—	—	—	—	—
Conflict resolution	—	—	—	—	—	—	—	—	—	—
Sexual fulfillment	—	—	—	—	—	—	—	—	—	—
Education and career development	—	—	—	—	—	—	—	—	—	—
Relationship with children	—	—	—	—	—	—	—	—	—	—
Relationship with grandchildren	—	—	—	—	—	—	—	—	—	—
Retirement plan	—	—	—	—	—	—	—	—	—	—
Relationship with aging parents	—	—	—	—	—	—	—	—	—	—

1. What are the best aspects of your marriage?
2. What are the areas that cause the greatest stress in your marriage?
3. What do you fear the most about your marriage in the future?
4. What are you looking forward to in your marriage in the future?

Surveying the Second Half of Marriage

Check your level of satisfaction in the following general categories as they relate to your marriage:

Areas of satisfaction or dissatisfaction:

	very dissatisfied			neither				very satisfied		
	1	2	3	4	5	6	7	8	9	10
Financial management	—	—	—	—	—	—	—	—	—	—
Companionship	—	—	—	—	—	—	—	—	—	—
Spiritual growth and commitment	—	—	—	—	—	—	—	—	—	—
Mutual activities	—	—	—	—	—	—	—	—	—	—
Individual activities	—	—	—	—	—	—	—	—	—	—
Communication with mate	—	—	—	—	—	—	—	—	—	—
My health and physical fitness	—	—	—	—	—	—	—	—	—	—
Mate's health and physical fitness	—	—	—	—	—	—	—	—	—	—
Ministry activities	—	—	—	—	—	—	—	—	—	—
Friends and extended family	—	—	—	—	—	—	—	—	—	—
Community service	—	—	—	—	—	—	—	—	—	—
Romance and intimacy	—	—	—	—	—	—	—	—	—	—
Household responsibilities	—	—	—	—	—	—	—	—	—	—
Conflict resolution	—	—	—	—	—	—	—	—	—	—
Sexual fulfillment	—	—	—	—	—	—	—	—	—	—
Education and career development	—	—	—	—	—	—	—	—	—	—
Relationship with children	—	—	—	—	—	—	—	—	—	—
Relationship with grandchildren	—	—	—	—	—	—	—	—	—	—
Retirement plan	—	—	—	—	—	—	—	—	—	—
Relationship with aging parents	—	—	—	—	—	—	—	—	—	—

1. What are the best aspects of your marriage?
2. What are the areas that cause the greatest stress in your marriage?
3. What do you fear the most about your marriage in the future?
4. What are you looking forward to in your marriage in the future?

Notes

PART ONE: GETTING READY FOR THE SECOND HALF

"Help! I'm Having a Midlife Marriage"

1. Georgia Witkin, "How to Keep Intimacy Alive," *Parade* (April 4, 1993), 12.

2. The Association for Couples in Marriage Enrichment (A.C.M.E.) is an international network of persons working for better marriages. Established in 1973, A.C.M.E. is a nonprofit, nonsectarian organization that promotes enrichment opportunities to help couples build on their strengths and equips them with skills and resources for a more satisfying relationship. There are local chapters in many communities, and there are more than three hundred leader couples throughout the U.S. and other countries who provide marriage enrichment activities. For more information about A.C.M.E.'s programs, leadership training, and publication, contact:

A.C.M.E.
P.O. Box 10596, Winston-Salem, NC 27108
(910) 724-1526 or 1-800-634-8325

3. David and Vera Mace, *Letters to a Retired Couple* (Valley Forge, Pa.: Judson, 1985), 37.

Surveying the Second Half of Marriage

1. Howard Whiteman, *Philadelphia Sunday Bulletin* (January 15, 1967).

2. Barbara Deane, *Getting Ready for a Great Retirement* (Colorado Springs: NavPress, 1992), 81.

PART TWO: FACING EIGHT MIDLIFE MARITAL CHALLENGES

Challenge One:
Let Go of Past Marital Disappointments, Forgive Each Other, and Commit to Making the Rest of Your Marriage the Best

1. David and Vera Mace, *We Can Have Better Marriages* (Nashville: Abingdon, 1974), 73.

Challenge Two:
Create a Marriage That Is Partner-Focused Rather Than Child-Focused

1. Judith Wallerstein and Sandra Blakeslee, *The Good Marriage* (Boston, New York: Houghton Mifflin, 1995), 62.

2. Gail Sheehy, *New Passages* (New York: Random House, 1995), 319.

3. David R. Mace, *Close Companions* (New York: Continuum, 1982), 92.

4. Ibid., 23. Throughout this book, we have used the terms "companionship," "partnership," and "partner-focused" interchangeably to describe the quality of relationship we are seeking to achieve in the second half of marriage. (While "companion" is a very broad word, when we apply it to the marriage relationship we mean partner, mate, friend, chum, buddy, as defined in *A Dictionary of Synonyms and Antonyms*.)

5. Scott M. Stanley, "Commitment Isn't Everything," *Marriage Partnership* (Spring 1996), 32.

6. Wallerstein and Blakeslee, *The Good Marriage*, 62.

7. Mace, *Close Companions*, 22.

8. Adapted from David and Vera Mace, *How to Have a Happy Marriage* (Nashville: Abingdon, 1977), 112–14.

Challenge Three:
Maintain an Effective Communication System That Allows You to Express Your Deepest Feelings, Joys, and Concerns

1. John A. Sanford, "Between People," *A.C.M.E. Newsletter* (October 1988).

2. Ray and Anne Ortlund, *The Best Half of Life* (Waco, Tex.: Word, 1976, 1988), 97.

3. John Gottman, *Why Marriages Succeed or Fail* (New York: Simon & Schuster, 1994), 29.

4. Ibid., 143–47.

5. Ibid.

6. Ibid.

7. Ibid.

8. Ibid., 209.

9. Ibid.

10. Mace, *Close Companions*, 20.

11. Ibid., 21.

Challenge Four:
Use Anger and Conflict in a Creative Way to Build Your Relationship

1. David Mace, "Love and Anger," *Family Life Today* (August 1983), 37.

2. Gottman, *Why Marriages Succeed or Fail*, 63.

3. Harriet Goldhor Lerner, *The Dance of Anger* (New York: Harper & Row, 1985), 4.

4. Ibid., 123–24.

5. Adapted from David and Vera Mace, *How to Have a Happy Marriage*, 112–14.

6. Ray and Anne Ortlund, *The Best Half of Life*, 100–101.

7. "Argue the Right Way and Keep Your Marriage Happy," *New Choices Magazine* (July-August 1994), 91. This study was funded by the National Institute on Aging and conducted by Robert Levenson, in collaboration with Laura Carstensen and John Gottman.

8. Ibid.

9. Wallerstein and Blakeslee, *The Good Marriage*, 146.

10. Adapted from David and Vera Mace, *How to Have a Happy Marriage*, 112–14.

Challenge Five:
Build a Deeper Friendship and Enjoy Your Spouse

1. Witkin, "How to Keep Intimacy Alive," 13.

2. Richard Matterson and Janis Long Harris, "What Kind of Friend Are You?" *Marriage Partnership* (Winter 1994), 51.

3. Ibid. Emphasis ours.

4. Adapted from Dave and Claudia Arp, *Fifty-two Dates for You and Your Mate* (Nashville: Nelson, 1993), 3 ff.

5. Dave and Claudia Arp, *The Ultimate Marriage Builder* (Nashville: Nelson, 1994), 199–200.

Challenge Six:
Renew Romance and Restore a Pleasurable Sexual Relationship

1. Gabriel Calvo, *Face to Face* (St. Paul, Minn.: Int. Marriage Encounter, 1988), 19.

2. Witkin, "How to Keep Intimacy Alive," 12.

3. Wallerstein and Blakeslee, *The Good Marriage*, 192.

4. Ibid.

5. David and Vera Mace, *Letters to a Retired Couple*, 70.

6. Edwin Kiester Jr. and Sally Valente Kiester, "Sex after Thirty-five— Why It's Different, Why It Can Be Better," *Readers Digest* (November 1995), 10–16. For a reprint of this article, write to Reprint Editor, Reader's Digest, Box 406, Pleasantville, NY 10570 and send five dollars.

7. Ibid.

8. Gail Sheehy, *New Passages*, 333.

9. David and Vera Mace, *Letters to a Retired Couple*, 74.

Challenge Seven:
Adjust to Changing Roles with Aging Parents and Adult Children

1. Gail Sheehy, *New Passages*, 49.
2. James Fairfield, *When You Don't Agree* (Scottdale, Pa.: Hearld, 1977), 56.
3. "Dear Abby," *Knoxville News-Sentinel* (November 19, 1995), E11.
4. David and Vera Mace, *Letters to a Retired Couple*, 112.

Challenge Eight:
Evaluate Where You Are on Your Spiritual Pilgrimage, Grow Closer to Each Other and to God, and Together Serve Others

1. Stephen G. Post, *Spheres of Love* (Dallas: Southern Methodist Press, 1994), 18–19.
2. *Seeds of Hope—A Henri Nouwen Reader*, ed. Robert Durback (New York: Bantam, 1989), 21.
3. Post, *Spheres of Love*, 18.
4. David and Vera Mace, *What's Happening to Clergy Marriages?* (Nashville: Abingdon, 1980), 100–103.
5. Paul Tournier, *To Understand Each Other* (Atlanta: John Knox, 1967), 58.
6. Ibid.
7. David and Vera Mace, *What's Happening to Clergy Marriages?* 99.
8. Ibid.
9. David and Vera Mace, *Marriage Enrichment in the Church* (Nashville: Broadman, 1976), 30–31. The Maces recommend John Howell's book *Equality and Submission in Marriage*, in which he has very ably and thoroughly explored the biblical and theological issues involved in marriage and has traced a continuum from the rigidly hierarchical pattern of marriage to the flexible companionship model, with the possibility of many variations along the line. All, he asserts, are options for the Christian couple.
10. Tournier, *To Understand Each Other*, 60.
11. David and Vera Mace, *What's Happening to Clergy Marriages?*, 103–4.
12. Dave and Claudia Arp, *The Marriage Track* (Nashville: Nelson, 1992), 182.
13. David and Vera Mace, *Letters to a Retired Couple*, 147.

PART THREE: THE STORY OF THE MCCRACKENS

Meet John and Sarah McCracken

1. David and Vera Mace, *We Can Have Better Marriages*, 66.

2. "What Is Marriage Enrichment?" *Marriage and Family Living* (May 1988), 31.

PART FOUR: THE MARRIAGE CHALLENGE

Challenge Your Marriage

1. David and Vera Mace, *Letters to a Retired Couple*, 26.

Acknowledgments

We wish to express our gratitude and thanks to:

- the people who participated in our Second Half of Marriage Survey. We appreciated your willingness to share the inside of your marriage—both your failures and your successes.
- the couples who have participated in our Marriage Alive Seminar over the years. Thank you for allowing us to tell your stories.
- our friends who our readers know as John and Sarah McCracken, for your willingness to share your journey into the second half of marriage—both your struggles and triumphs—so we could pass your gift of encouragement and hope on to others.
- our dear friend and mentor, Vera Mace, for your and David's life work in helping marriages succeed, for introducing the concept of marriage enrichment, and for your input, wisdom, and insight in helping us with this book.
- our pastor, John Wood, for your biblical input and theological soundness, and for your and Marianne's friendship and encouragement over the years.
- our friend and publisher, Scott Bolinder, whose belief in us and vision for this book turned a dream into reality. You never know who you are going to meet in an elevator. Scott, we are glad we met you!
- our editor, Sandy Vander Zicht, for sharing your expertise with us, for patiently pushing us toward excellence, and Bob Hudson and Robin Schmitt for your excellent editing.

- to Lisa Guest for her clear and thought-provoking writing.
- to our own Arp "in house" team—Jonathan and Autumn Whiteman Arp for tabulating our survey and putting the results in a format that is easy to understand, and Laurie Clark for your expertise in helping us transform our passion for helping long-term marriages into logical chapters that relay the message to our readers.
- to the many researchers and authors from whom we quoted, for your sound work that gives a solid base for the cause of marriage enrichment.
- to our literary agent, Greg Johnson of Alive Communications, for being our advocate, and encouraging us along the way.

Discussion Guide

written by Lisa Guest

☙

To the Discussion Leader

The Second Half of Marriage discussion guide is set up as a thirteen-week study. It can, however, be approached in a variety of ways. An eight-week study would offer a survey of the eight challenges. Participants in a four-week series could discuss two challenges per session.

Whatever approach you choose, keep in mind that far more important than covering all the material in each section is meeting the needs of group members. Be sensitive to the issues and questions that are most important to them. Also be sensitive to how open they want to be about the very personal aspects of their marriage, and remind them at the beginning of each session that they will not be required to share their responses. We encourage you, especially during the first few meetings, to focus on the less personal questions for group discussion. But be sure to have group members write down their answers to the personal application questions and, ideally, discuss them with their spouse before the meeting so that they will benefit more from the large group discussion.

During your times together, we ask that you, as the leader, make sure that everyone has the opportunity to participate. Be careful not to let discussions become problem-solving sessions focused on one person's or couple's unique situation. Try to emphasize general principles and common struggles so that everyone attending can benefit and learn. Also be sure that everyone understands the importance of confidentiality: everything shared in the group is to stay in the group.

We also ask that, as the group leader, you begin each session with a brief reference to what was discussed the time before and use that to build a bridge to the discussion that is about to begin. Before starting to talk about challenge 2, for instance, refer back to the previous discussion about the importance of forgiveness in a marriage: "The topic of this session may give you the opportunity to practice that forgiveness as we talk about moving from a marriage that has been too child-focused to a marriage that is partner-focused." Depending on how much time you and the group decide to spend together each session, you could open each meeting with a general "How's it going?" question or by asking something like "What did you try to live out from our discussion last time—and what happened in your marriage as a result?" and then make the transition to the discussion ahead.

Finally, we encourage individuals, couples, and group leaders alike to begin their preparation time and their discussion time with prayer. After all, God alone can transform hearts and therefore marriages, so be sure to involve him in this exciting, life-changing process.

Session 1:
Introduction

❧

1. Why are you reading this book? What (or who!) compelled you to open its cover?

2. What do you hope to gain from working through the challenges you'll find in the pages of this book? Be specific about problems to be solved, issues to be worked through, and goals to be reached.

3. Before going any farther, identify where you are in your marriage. How long have you been married? How old are your children? Your parents? Who lives at home with you and your mate? Why would you say that you are in (or approaching) "the second half of marriage"?

4. Once their boys were out of the house, the Arps say, "We went from a child-centered marriage to an activity-centered one, still with little time and energy for each other" (p. 11). Is your marriage child-centered? Activity-centered? Or focused on something else? On a scale of 1 to 5, how satisfied are you with the amount of time and energy you have for each other? Let 1 be "very dissatisfied" and 5 be "very satisfied." Identify what keeps you from having the time and energy you want to have for one another.

5. Spend a few moments praying together. You might close with the following prayer.

Lord God, you were the One who brought us together. We ask for your bless-ing on our marriage and the work we will be doing together to strengthen it. Enable both of us to be open, honest, and vulnerable, sensitive when it's our turn to speak and accepting when it's our turn to listen. Please use this book and the thoughts and discussions it sparks to change our hearts, renew our love for each other, and thereby transform our marriage. Amen.

SESSION 2:
"Help! I'm Having a Midlife Marriage"

1. With what thoughts and feelings have you faced—or do you anticipate—the empty nest?

2. Look again at the section entitled "Beginning the Second Half," especially the second paragraph. In what details do you see your-selves? In what direction did you move (or might you move) after years of being child-focused in your marriage? If your children have already moved out, did you become partner-focused or activity-focused? What red flags about the state of your relation-ship, if any, did you notice at that time?

3. Take some time to evaluate your marriage. List the marriage assets and the marriage liabilities as you see them.

4. Having taken a somewhat objective look at your marriage, consider the following three questions.

- What can you do to maximize your assets and minimize your liabilities?

- What are your dreams—both individually and as a couple?

- In light of those dreams, what specific goals will you set for yourselves?

5. How do you define "finishing well" for your marriage? Be as specific as possible. Then, as you consider what you want your marriage to look like in its second half, find a couple who can be a model and, perhaps, even be a mentor for your marriage.

6. Are you willing to take the risk to grow together in your marriage so that the second half is far better than the first half? Are you willing to make yourself more vulnerable to your spouse, rearrange your schedule, learn new skills, and/or change some personal habits? Are you willing to create a relationship that preserves the best from the first half of your marriage but at the same time offers you the freedom to adapt and grow in new ways? If you can answer yes to these questions, what is motivating that desire? If you are answering no, what is causing your hesitation?

SESSION 3:
Surveying the Second Half of Marriage

1. To what do you attribute the fact that divorce among thirty-years-plus marriages is increasing?

2. To evaluate more closely your marriage, complete the Second Half of Marriage survey if you haven't already (see Appendix).

   • What surprised you about what you learned from the surveys?

   • What did the survey reveal to you about the level of expectations you and your mate have for specific aspects of your marriage? (Low ratings can indicate high expectations; high ratings can indicate low expectations.)

3. Review the eight challenges outlined on pages 42–45. At this point, which challenge seems most daunting?

4. Now take time to answer some or all of the questions in the Marriage Builder "Reflecting on My Marriage" (p. 46). Some of these you have already touched on; others introduce new topics.

5. Having looked at your marriage, what little steps—what unselfish choice, what forgiveness, what act of kindness, what extra effort—can you take today to help build a healthy marriage?

SESSION 4:
Challenge One

Let Go of Past Marital Disappointments, Forgive Each Other, and Commit to Making the Rest of Your Marriage the Best

✌

1. What specific events or ongoing situations came to mind when you first read "let go of past marital disappointments"? ... With what emotions or thoughts did you respond to the call to "forgive each other"? ...

2. Make an "I'll Never Do" list. Then discuss what is freeing about seeing in writing this list of dreams and goals that you will not be able to realize or accomplish.

3. Why is forgiveness key to a healthy marriage relationship?

4. Consider two rules for the second half shared by a couple who have faced a medical crisis. Rule 1 is "Don't sweat the small stuff." Rule 2 is "Everything is small stuff." What benefits can come from holding this perspective?

5. The Arps suggest two important steps to forgiveness (p. 57). Their friend Jennifer lived out those steps and, as a result, came to treasure her marriage, one that was better in the second half

than the first. Discuss Jennifer's approach to marriage. What principles did she follow? What benefits did she enjoy as a result?

—*Decide to forgive.* If you haven't already, take some time now to personalize the process by walking through the steps described on pages 58–60.

—*Don't limit forgiveness.*

- What keeps you from being generous with forgiveness?

- What keeps you from asking for forgiveness when appropriate?

- Look closely at Colossians 3:12–14 for qualities needed if you are to swat at the gnats in your marriage without swatting each other. Why are compassion and kindness— as well as acceptance and forgiveness—vital in a healthy, growing marriage? In what specific aspects of your marriage do you need to extend compassion to your mate? Kindness?

- What do humility, gentleness, and patience contribute to a marriage? Identify where in your marriage you need to exercise these virtues.

6. Wherever you are in your marriage today, will you renew your commitment to your mate and make a commitment to grow together for the second half of your marriage? If you aren't ready to say yes, discover why, review God's intentions for marriage ("till death do us part"), and pray that God will transform your heart and fill it with a new love for your spouse.

7. If you are ready to renew your commitment to your marriage, write out that commitment in the form of a letter or a list of "Things I Will Do in the Second Half of Marriage" and tell your mate about your renewed commitment to him or her.

8. If you haven't already done so, write out your answers to each of the six questions on pages 64–65. After you have done that, look back at your answers. What do your answers reveal about the kind of marriage partner you are? Which answers help you step into your spouse's shoes—and what do you see differently from that perspective? According to your answers, what aspects of your marriage need some focused prayer and effort?

SESSION 5:
Challenge Two

Create a Marriage That Is Partner-Focused Rather Than Child-Focused

ᴈᴇ

1. What model(s) of a partner-focused marriage do you have in your life?

2. What crises have you weathered on your marital roller coaster? To what or whom do you attribute your ability to do so?

3. What might be some effective ways of coping with the woman's shift from nurturing to being more interested in tasks and accomplishments, just as the man shifts from being work-oriented to being more expressive and emotionally responsive?

4. What can block intimacy in the second half of marriage? What, if anything, is blocking intimacy between you and your mate?

5. How can a traditional style of marriage (characterized by a "divide and conquer" approach to responsibilities) block intimacy?

6. How can a companionship style of marriage (characterized by an effort to share responsibility, decision making, and parenting) foster intimacy?

7. Where do you and your spouse fall on the continuum between a traditional and a companionship marriage? Support your answer with specific details about your interactions. Then comment on the degree of intimacy you share and how satisfied you are with it. Don't be afraid to say, "Things are crummy right now. This is not what I want for our marriage. Let's start getting to know each other again."

8. In what ways do you put your marriage first? How do you use your diversity to create couple unity? Be specific about the effort and the outcome.

9. Critical to the second half of marriage is developing a sense of we-ness. What can you do to develop we-ness and focus on your spouse?

10. Why does it make sense that the quest for intimacy in a companionship marriage leads to a degree of closeness that can generate conflict? What are some ways companionship couples might defuse that conflict?

11. The transition to a companionship marriage in the second half of marriage is like the transition from piston-engine planes to jet-engine planes. Retraining is necessary if you are to enjoy flying higher and faster in your marriage. And Drs. David and Vera Mace offer three essentials to such flying (p. 79).

    • *A commitment to growth.* Why is this key to second-half marriages? What risk does this commitment involve?

    • *An effectively functioning communication system.* What can and should be different about communication in the second half of marriage versus communication in the first half of marriage? Why can that change be threatening?

    • *The ability to make creative use of conflict.* How can love *and* anger be positive forces in building a healthy marriage? (You'll look at this more closely in challenge 4.)

12. Talk with your mate about the opportunities for growth you are facing in your marriage right now. As a couple, how will you respond to those opportunities?

SESSION 6:
Challenge Three

Maintain an Effective Communication System That Allows You to Express Your Deepest Feelings, Joys, and Concerns

1. Which universal conversation blockers—time crunch, work overload, a stressful lifestyle, parenting, extended family responsibilities, sports and hobbies, television—have you encountered? What conversation blockers, if any, can you add to this list?

2. What ways of communicating that were necessary and perhaps even effective when kids were around aren't so effective now and instead point to some "apartness" in your second-half-of-marriage relationship?

3. The healthiest communication pattern is the style of an interpersonally competent couple. This style builds on a desire for companionship and we-ness; it transcends your own tendency, cultural conditioning, or personality. Work through the following seven tips for talking on a more personal level.

   • *Learn to listen.* Who in your life is a good listener? What characterizes him or her? Also, what should you be listening for when your spouse speaks? Why?

- *Be aware of the nonverbal message.* When has a nonverbal message been louder and contradictory to the verbal message you were given? What does your spouse do to communicate nonverbally? What do you do?

- *Learn to communicate your feelings.* Do you struggle to share positive feelings, negative feelings, or both? Does your spouse?

- *Use "I" statements; avoid "you" statements and "why" questions.* Why are "I" statements more effective than "you" statements and "why" questions? As you answer, think about how you respond to comments like "You always ignore me. Why don't you ever talk with me?" Then think back on your communication in the preceding week. Do you remember making more "I" statements or more "you" statements? What does your answer show you about yourself?

- *Learn to complete the communication cycle.* Explain what the communication cycle is and give an example of how it works. How do you or would you respond to this kind of reflecting back? Why is this key to becoming more intimate?

- *Agree not to attack the other person or to defend yourself.* Why does this agreement foster intimacy? What will you do to overcome the urge to attack your spouse or defend yourself the next time you disagree? What will you do to not arouse in your spouse the urge to attack or become defensive? Be specific and practical on both counts.

- *Have regular couple-communication times.* What problems can be prevented by having a daily time when spouses touch base? What do you need to do to make such a time happen?

Consider the need to reschedule, reorganize a routine, or even find the energy and desire for such communication.

4. Discuss what it means to speak the truth in love (Eph. 4:15). Describe the approach you would appreciate if someone needed to speak a hard-to-hear truth to you. How closely does your usual style with your mate match that approach?

Session 7:
Challenge Four

Use Anger and Conflict in a Creative Way to Build Your Relationship

✢

1. What have you learned about how to handle light turbulence? Moderate turbulence? What do you do to preserve the relationship and incur no structural damage to your marriage?

2. An enriched marriage is a lifetime commitment followed by daily commitments to put marriage first and personal wishes and rights second. For the Arps, that means copiloting. Would you say that you and your mate are copilots? If so, what direction have you agreed to head in? How do you resolve differences of opinion? What do you do to cope with the fewer defined roles and the blurred division of responsibilities that come in the second half of marriage?

3. Marital turbulence (a.k.a. arguing) needs to be handled with care that negative feelings are expressed in a positive way. Each partner must first deal with his or her own anger. Review the questions at the top of page 109. What benefits come from answering those questions before approaching your spouse?

4. Once you have processed your anger individually, you can and should process anger as a couple. Look again at the anger contract on page 110. Why is having an anger contract a good idea?

5. As the Marriage Builder on page 116 asks, how do you currently handle anger? How would you like to handle anger? Will you and your spouse sign the anger contract? Why or why not?

6. Constructive arguing can enrich your marriage. That kind of arguing is characterized by staying focused on the issue, using signs of affection to defuse anger, and adding a touch of humor (not sarcasm!). What can these three points do to enrich a marriage as you resolve conflicts?

7. To pull together several aspects of this section, work through the Marriage Builder on page 115 if you haven't already. What do your answers show you about yourself? Where do you need to grow? What will you do to encourage that growth in yourself?

SESSION 8:
Challenge Five

Build a Deeper Friendship
and Enjoy Your Spouse

ℜ

1. How much time do you and your mate spend together on a given day? In a given week? What can you do to be more intentional about spending time together?

2. What activities do you enjoy—or might you enjoy—doing together? Make a list and then choose one idea from your list and make a date. (If you need ideas, look again at the Marriage Alive answers on pp. 123–24. The Marriage Builder on p. 131 can help, too.)

3. Review the following six tips for living a more balanced and healthier life and let them serve as a mirror for you.

   • *Take care of yourself.* When did you last have a physical? Evaluate the quality of your diet. Are you getting the exercise you need?

   • *Pace yourself.* What changes do you need to make in order to live a healthier (i.e., slower, simpler) pace? Make them!

- *Build relationships and maintain them.* Why do friends make life more balanced and healthier? What friendships will you work to rebuild? What new friendships will you pursue?

- *Stretch your boundaries.* Why can stretched boundaries add fun to your friendship? What new things have you tried or could you try together? Go for it!

- *Stay involved with life.* Why is staying involved in life important to a healthy marriage? What are some ways second-halfers can stay involved in life? What are some of your ways? What is your passion? What risks are you taking? What are you learning?

- *Hang in there.* Why does change need to be embraced? Why can the fact that life is full of changes be a real encouragement? What changes do you need to embrace?

4. Key to Lucy and William's long-term friendship during their fifty-plus years of marriage are praying together and dating. Why can prayer strengthen a friendship? When do (or could) you and your mate pray together regularly? What can a regular dating life do for a marriage? When was your last date—and when is your next date? Put it on the calendar, and if you need ideas, choose from the list on pages 129–30.

5. Use the Marriage Builder on page 132 and plan the ultimate date. Then enjoy the weekend getaway-for-two you plan!

SESSION 9:
Challenge Six

Renew Romance and Restore
a Pleasurable Sexual Relationship

⤫

1. Fanning the flame and stoking the fire of your love life takes effort and time. What does your calendar/planner reveal about the priority of your love relationship with your spouse? What specifically can you do to find more time for each other and make that relationship a priority?

2. Researcher Judith Wallerstein claims that "a richly rewarding and stable sex life is . . . the central task of marriage" (p. 138). Why does she say that? Do you agree with her? Why or why not?

3. David and Vera Mace maintain that "attitude" is key to a fulfilled sexual relationship. What is a healthy and appropriate attitude toward sexuality in the second half of marriage?

4. Review the five suggestions for enhancing your love life for the second half (see pp. 141–42). What did you learn from these suggestions (discussed more fully on pp. 141–42)? What suggestion(s) will you try? Which one will you begin working on this week?

    *   Look again at six secrets for rekindling romance (see pp. 145–48) and discuss each with your mate.

1. *Be affectionate.* What actions best communicate affection to you? What actions speak of your affection most clearly to your spouse?

2. *Be a listener.* Why are listening with your heart and talking to your spouse while you are loving each other two of the most important lovemaking skills and romance enhancers?

3. *Be adventuresome.* What elements of adventure could a second-half couple add to their lovemaking?

4. *Be playful.* What kind of play can add romance to lovemaking?

5. *Be in shape.* What kind of getting- and staying-in-shape activities can a second-half couple share?

6. *Be a little wacky.* Shakertown isn't an option for everyone, but what types of wackiness are?

- Which of these six secrets will you try this week? Which might you ask your mate to try?

- Do the Marriage Builder "Let's Talk about Sex" (p. 150). As you talk, keep in mind that couples who stay sexually and emotionally intimate during the second half of marriage are, according to Georgia Witkin, stubbornly determined to stay that way despite changes and challenges (p. 137). Use this discussion as an opportunity to express and strengthen that determination.

SESSION 10:

Challenge Seven

Adjust to Changing Roles with Aging Parents and Adult Children

1. Describe your family seesaw. What adolescent or adult children and maybe grandchildren are on one end, and whose aging parents are on the other end? What kind of balancing act do these two ends of the seesaw demand?

2. Which of the following typical problems prevent a healthy relationship with your parents?

   • Their failure to trust you

   • Their failure to grant you adult status

   • Denial and little honest communication

   • Excessive demands and manipulation

3. Whatever your relationship with your parents, describe how you are balancing the biblical instruction to leave your mother and father and cleave to your mate with the biblical instruction to honor your mother and father.

4. Which of the following might you do to strengthen your marriage even as you care for your parents?

- Look for the positive in your relationship with your parents.

- Build positive bridges by collecting family history or family wisdom.

- Express positive feelings to your parents, based on the Marriage Builder on page 100.

- Do something out of character.

- Do something they want to do.

- Provide lots of pictures.

5. Which of these tips do you need to act on to build your marriage?

- *Deal with false guilt.* What is false guilt? How can a person identify it?

- *Don't feel responsible for what you can't control.* What things are beyond your control?

- *Get advice from others.* Whom can you go to for advice?

- *Get a life.* As you consider your current situation, what does this phrase mean to you? What changes does it call you to make?

6. Relating to adult children and their spouses can be a difficult challenge. What, if anything, did you realize about yourself and some changes that need to be made, after reading the section entitled "A View from the Other Side" (p. 162)?

7. Which of the following may you be guilty of—and what will you do to change?

   - Failure to trust your children

   - Failure to give your adult children adult status

   - Interfering instead of respecting your children's boundaries

8. Review the tips offered by married adult children and listed on page 164. Which tips do you need to hear—and which will you start acting on now?

9. To further clarify your understanding of your relationship with your adult children, do the Marriage Builder on page 169.

SESSION *11:*
Challenge Eight

Evaluate Where You Are on Your Spiritual Pilgrimage, Grow Closer to Each Other and to God, and Together Serve Others

❧

1. After reading this chapter, explain in your own words what the phrase "sacred canopy of marriage" means to you (see p. 174).

2. Review the Maces' five core beliefs about marriage (pp. 176–77). Which ones can you affirm as your own beliefs? Which ones, if any, give you pause? What will you do to work through your hesitation about those?

3. In what specific ways can and should a couple's faith in God and beliefs about Christian marriage make a radical difference in their relationship with their spouse?

4. The spiritual pilgrimages of both the husband and wife determine the quality of their relationship to one another, so consider these three suggestions for continuing your spiritual journey together.

    —*Accept where you both are on your spiritual journey.*

    • Individually and as a couple, where are you on your spiritual pilgrimage?

- Most couples are at different places individually. How can you let that diversity enrich your relationship rather than divide you?

- Review the Arps' discussion of three tips for your spiritual journey (p. 181) and then ask God to help you accept where you and your spouse are on that journey.

—Promote spiritual closeness.

- How do you define spiritual closeness?

- What can you do to promote spiritual closeness with God? With your spouse?

- Are you willing to try the ten-minute miracle and pray with your spouse daily (pp. 181–82)? If your spouse agrees, you two might want to choose a mutual friend to hold you accountable and, even better, join you in the miracle!

- Are you interested in trying the Quaker tradition of sharing silence (p. 182)? Again, if your spouse agrees, you might want to establish a system for accountability.

—Together serve others.

- What are you doing to serve God?

- What can you do to love and serve your spouse?

- What can you do together to serve God? Be specific as you make your list. Then choose one item and do it! If you need ideas, call your pastor.

SESSION 12:
Meet John and Sarah McCracken

❧

1. What value is there in looking at other marriages, especially those who have covered ground you have yet to cover? What real-life models for marriage—particularly second-half marriage—do you have? How have you benefited?

2. In what ways, if any, did John's wake-up call speak to you? Have you ever felt on the outside of your family and been left, figuratively speaking, holding the garbage?

3. At what points can you relate to Sarah's initial sharing (pp. 190–91)? Be specific.

4. Shortly after their nest became empty, John and Sarah discovered that the second half of marriage is a very personal stage of life—and that neither of them handled the personal side of life very well (p. 192). What do you think makes the second half so personal? How well do you think you handle the personal side of life? Explain your answer.

5. What helped you realize that you needed new skills for your empty nest—and what were those skills?

6. What roles did you and your spouse assume in the first half? What does the second half call for?

7. Make a list of your interests and have your spouse do the same. What do you have in common? If it appears that you have nothing in common (the McCrackens' lists were quite different!), work together to identify some common ground. Developing shared interests may not be easy, but it is key to strengthening your marriage.

8. What do you and your spouse do for fun? What elements of the unexpected have you or could you introduce to your daily life? What can you do to be less predictable?

9. John McCracken says that "the essence of love is trying to understand your mate" (p. 204). What would you say is the essence of love?

10. When John gave up the idea of a perfect marriage, he says he "began to realize we could have a growing one" (p. 204). Why is a growing marriage a better alternative?

   • Look again at the McCrackens' letter (pp. 205–6). What encouragement do you find in their words? Which of their three discoveries—"we *should* change and *could* change"; "we had to relearn how to listen to each other"; and "we feel we have reshaped ... our marriage ... in a manner compatible with this stage of life"—is important for your current situation? Finally, will you accept the Arps' challenge to grow in the second half of your marriage as the McCrackens did? More to come on that in the final chapter.

SESSION *13:*
Challenge Your Marriage

1. Consider again the story of the Arps' ficus tree and how it offers a picture of the kind of growing you can choose to do in your second-half marriage.

    • What sense of being uprooted have you experienced during your second half?

    • What negative habits and patterns have you chosen and/or are you choosing to uproot?

    • In what healthy soil are you replanting your perhaps rootbound marriage?

2. What changes have you experienced in the last decade of your marriage?

3. What changes do you anticipate in the next ten years? What are you or could you be doing, if anything, to prepare yourself for those changes?

4. What new habits are you willing to develop to replace those negative ones you have uprooted and to foster positive change in your marriage?

5. The Arps write, "So many times we see that it's not a matter of knowing what to do but doing what we know" (p. 211). What does this statement mean to you today? What encouragement to act do you find in it? Be as specific as possible.

6. Having almost completed your study of *The Second Half of Marriage*, develop a plan for accountability so your growth can continue. With whom will you share this book and commit to work on the eight challenges? Who might you invite to join a supper club? With whom could you share the *10 Great Dates* book and/or video series? See p. 256 for more information. The support of some couple friends who are in or about to enter the second half of marriage can be invaluable to your ongoing journey.

   • To wrap up your study of the eight challenges of marriage—and to fuel your growth in each of these eight areas—work through the Marriage Builder "Challenging Your Marriage" on page 214. Be open and honest as you consider where you are growing, where you still need to grow, and where you can contribute to meeting each challenge.

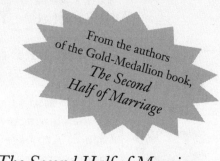

From the authors of the Gold-Medallion book, *The Second Half of Marriage*

The Second Half of Marriage
Zondervan*Groupware*™

Facing the Eight Challenges
of the Empty-Nest Years
David & Claudia Arp

A small group video curriculum designed for empty nesters ... and all long-term marriages.

The children are gone or are leaving soon. Now, it's time to focus on the future and especially the marriage. The second half of a marriage can be a time of incredible fulfillment, no matter what challenges a couple previously faced. Couples can rediscover each other and build a more mature, satisfying, and romantic live together. *The Second Half of Marriage* Zondervan*Groupware*™ kit is an effective means for promoting discussion between couples because it is:

• Easy to lead
• Flexible
• Lively
• Interactive
• Great for small groups, seminars, and retreats

The Second Half of Marriage Zondervan*Groupware*™ is a unique resource designed to facilitate rediscovery and rebuilding. It challenges couples to shape a vision for the rest of their life together and encourages them to develop a creative approach to make that vision a reality.

ISBN 0-310-23684-3

Also Available Separately:
Leader's Guide: 0-310-23687-8
Participant's Guide: 0-310-23761-0
Softcover Book: 0-310-21935-3

ZONDERVAN™

GRAND RAPIDS, MICHIGAN 49530

WWW.ZONDERVAN.COM

Ten Fun-Filled Dates That
Will Revitalize Your Marriage!

10 Great Dates to Revitalize Your Marriage
David & Claudia Arp

Dating doesn't have to be only a memory or just another boring evening at the movies. David and Claudia Arp have revolutionized dating by creating ten memory-making evenings built on key, marriage-enriching themes. This approach to relationship growth involves both partners, is low-key, and best of all, is exciting, proven, and FUN!

Draw upon the best tips from David and Claudia Arp's popular Marriage Alive Seminars in this book, *10 Great Dates*. You'll learn how to:

- Communicate better
- Build a creative sex life
- Process anger and resolve conflicts
- Develop spiritual intimacy
- Balance busy lifestyles
- And more!

Softcover 0-310-21091-7

Also look for ...
10 Great Dates to Revitalize Your Marriage Video Curriculum

This video curriculum is based on the Marriage Alive Seminars and the *10 Great Dates to Revitalize Your Marriage* book.

The curriculum kit contains:
- two 75-minute videos with ten short date launches
- one *10 Great Dates to Revitalize Your Marriage* softcover (208 pages)
- one Leader's Guide (48 pages)

Softcover 0-310-21350-9

ZONDERVAN™

GRAND RAPIDS, MICHIGAN 49530

WWW.ZONDERVAN.COM